Maternal and Infant Assessment for Breastfeeding and Human Lactation

Maternal and Infant Assessment for Breastfeeding and Human Lactation

A Guide for the Practitioner

Karin Cadwell

Cynthia Turner-Maffei

Barbara O'Connor

Anna Blair

JONES AND BARTLETT PUBLISHERS

Sudbury, Massachusetts

BOSTON   TORONTO   LONDON   SINGAPORE

World Headquarters
Jones and Bartlett Publishers
40 Tall Pine Drive
Sudbury, MA 01776
978-443-5000
info@jbpub.com
www.jbpub.com

Jones and Bartlett Publishers Canada
2406 Nikanna Road
Mississauga, ON
CANADA
L5C 2W6

Jones and Bartlett Publishers International
Barb House, Barb Mews
London W6 7PA
UK

Copyright © 2002 by Jones and Bartlett Publishers, Inc.

ISBN 0-7637-2097-6

Library of Congress Cataloging-in-Publication Data
CIP data unavailable at time of printing.

Acquisitions Editor: Penny M. Glynn
Associate Editor: Thomas Prindle
Production Manager: Amy Rose
Manufacturing Buyer: Amy Duddridge
Typesetting: Carlisle Publishers Services
Text Design: Anne Spencer
Cover Design: Philip Regan
Printing and Binding: Courier Stoughton

Printed in the United States of America
05 04 03 02 01   10 9 8 7 6 5 4 3 2 1

About the Authors

Karin Cadwell, PhD, RN, IBCLC is a nationally and internationally recognized speaker, researcher, educator and faculty member of the Healthy Children 2000 Project, Inc. She convened Baby-Friendly USA, implementing the UNICEF Baby-Friendly Hospital Initiative in the United States, and was a visiting professor and program chair of the Health Communications Department of Emerson College. She is a member of the U.S. Breastfeeding Committee, is a member of the Board of Directors of Healthy Mothers/Healthy Babies and former Chair of the National Healthy Mothers/Healthy Babies Breastfeeding Committee, and has led the Eisenhower Foundation annual international PTP delegation on breastfeeding and human lactation exchanges to other nations. She is the author of numerous books and articles, was awarded the designation IBCLC in 1985 for "significant contribution to the field," and has since recertified by exam.

Cynthia Turner-Maffei, MA, IBCLC is the national coordinator of Baby-Friendly USA, a faculty member of the Healthy Children 2000 Project, Inc., and adjunct faculty member, of the Union Institute. She has extensive experience as a nutritionist and breastfeeding educator in WIC and other Maternal Child Health programs. A member of breastfeeding coalitions on the local, state, and national levels, including the Massachusetts Breastfeeding Committee and the U.S. Breastfeeding Committee, she is also an author of *The Curriculum to Support the Ten Steps to Successful Breastfeeding* and *Toward Evidence-Based Breastfeeding Practice.*

Barbara O'Connor, RN, BSN, IBCLC holds degrees in nursing and elementary education. As a faculty member of the Healthy Children 2000 Project, Inc., Barbara teaches lactation counselor programs both nationally and internationally. Barbara has extensive experience in developing and implementing adolescent and adult peer education/support programs. She has worked in a variety of settings as a newborn nursery nurse, school nurse, HIV/AIDS educator, and WIC Coordinator. Barbara is active in several task forces. She was a member of the first International People to People Breastfeeding and Human Lactation delegations to Russia, Romania, and Cuba.

Anna Blair, PhD, CLC is a faculty member of the Healthy Children 2000 Project, Inc., and has focused her work primarily on evidence-based practice, ethics, and teamwork with maternal and child health in the area of community and hospital-based work groups and task forces. Her master's degree is in Organizational Behavior. Studying Health Communications at the Union Institute, Anna's doctoral work resulted in research relating the positioning of the baby at the breast to breast and nipple soreness in the mother. She was one of the worldwide coordinators for the GLOPAR project. She is the co-author of *Toward Evidence–Based Breastfeeding Practice.*

Acknowledgments

We are grateful for the support, shared insight, and input of our families; our colleagues at the Center for Breastfeeding: Lois Arnold, Elyse Blair, Gail Steibel Douma, Laura Engvall, Vanessa Ford, Deborah Krauter, Nikki Lee, Whitney Mirvis, Debi Sines Pancoe, Debbie Pierce, Sally Syrjala, and Dawn Tardif; as well as our colleagues in the larger lactation community, notably Sarah Coulter Danner, Chloe Fisher, Kittie Frantz, Peter Hartmann, Elisabet Helsing, Kay Hoover, Eutedrah Hutchinson-Burnett, Marshall Klaus, Ruth Lawrence, Chele Marmet, Gro Nylander, Lennart Righard, Ellen Shell, Linda J. Smith, Kerstin Uvnäs-Moberg, and Ann-Marie Widström.

This book also had a wonderful midwife in Kajsa Brimdyr, PhD, to whom we owe our thanks and gratitude for her organizational and technical assistance.

Special thanks to all the mothers and babies with whom we have been honored to work, and to the participants of our training programs for providing the impetus and renewed energy to continue the quest to truly understand the life-giving, rapturous dance of the nursing mother and babe.

Introduction

Those who assist breastfeeding mothers and babies come from a broad range of educational backgrounds—from physicians, peer counselors, occupational therapists, nurses, and social workers, to high school graduates and post-graduate researchers. This richness of experience and viewpoint brings with it inherent challenges. There is no one, common "language" spoken, no sole lexicon, and limited agreement regarding the etiology of problems. There are varied scopes of practice and different comfort levels with technology, terminology, and intervention strategies. This text strives to provide a center point for understanding the physical and behavioral contributions of the mother and infant to the breastfeeding relationship.

The diversity and scope of practice for breastfeeding assessors presents some limitations to the assessment process. For example, the professional practice scope of many of those who assist breastfeeding families does not include tactile intraoral examination of the infant or tactile examination of the breasts. For this reason, this text explores hallmarks of breastfeeding problems that can be seen, heard, or otherwise observed without further physical examination. When hallmarks of problems are discovered, the assessor should immediately refer the mother/infant to the appropriate healthcare provider for further evaluation, diagnosis, and treatment. Many problems that appear as breastfeeding problems may actually be symptoms of more deeply seated medical problems.

Most mothers and infants don't have medical problems. However, all assessors should be prepared to distinguish among breastfeeding problems, breastfeeding problems that are actually medical problems, and medical problems. Assessment offers insight into the integrity and interplay of the maternal and infant physical systems. Feeding is perhaps the most intense interchange between caregivers and infants in the first months of life, encompassing two or more hours face-to-face daily. Because of the range of maternal/infant systems involved in lactation and feeding, we cannot underestimate the potential for discovering a variety of physical challenges. The assessment of breastfeeding mothers and infants requires developing a broad and comprehensive view of the multi-factoral components of successful breastfeeding.

It is our hope that this text will provide a framework upon which assessors can construct a well-rounded process for determining the breastfeeding status of the mothers and infants with whom they work. Assessment is one of the most important skill sets of those who assist breastfeeding families. This book will not serve well as a "cookbook" for solving problems. It is intended to be used in conjunction with other resources to expand the assessor's knowledge and management of breastfeeding. Because it is inherently difficult to tease breastfeeding problems apart to their infant and maternal origins, there is some overlap of the material of many chapters. This text can assist the assessor in seeking clues to the identification of the factors contributing to the challenges at hand and, thus, to the construction of tailored solutions to each situation. Assessment skills need a firm foundation as well as continuous updating and expansion. Knowledge about breastfeeding and human lactation is constantly expanding. The assessor's conceptual framework must be both broad and deep.

Because of the complex nature of the breastfeeding mother and infant, the assessor is reminded to practice the art of detection in approaching breastfeeding problems. Breastfeeding problems rarely have one cause. There are many possible contributory factors interwoven in the maternal and infant breastfeeding systems. It is essential to understand the optimal process of breastfeeding in order to discern those characteristics of feeding that are less than optimal. Breastfeeding problems that sound similar to others seen by the assessor in the past may have a completely different etiology. While past experience with similar cases can provide some direction for exploration, good assessment demands thorough examination of the unique aspects of the new situation. Rather than relying on past experience, the assessor should strive to see each mother/infant pair as a new mystery to be solved.

This book springs from our experience in developing a course on assessment of the mother and infant in conjunction with the undergraduate and graduate degree programs in human lactation developed by the Healthy Children 2000 Project, Inc., the Union Institute, and Goddard College with partial funding support from the United States Health Resources Services Administration's Maternal and Child Health Bureau. As we began to develop the framework for the assessment course (one of several courses developed for the degree programs), we searched for a text that would meet the anticipated needs of learners. We found that classic texts on maternal and infant assessment contained too little information on the unique characteristics of the breastfeeding mother and infant, focusing primarily on what is known about the bottlefed infant. Turning to the lactation texts, we found that there were excellent pieces of helpful material sprinkled throughout many of the existing texts, but there was no one book that encompassed the material we envisioned. This book strives to elaborate upon the unique components of the breastfeeding mother/infant dyad and provide this essential material in a single source.

How to Use This Book

This book is organized into four major areas:

Within Sections I through III, the optimal components of breastfeeding are presented, followed by a discussion of possible deviations from the norm. The text is illustrated with 78 figures. Line art appears in the body of the chapter, while photographs appear in the color plate insert at the back of the book.

Throughout the text, icons are used to denote how the information discussed may be gathered.

Method	Symbol	How these clues may be gathered
Careful look		Looking closely
Interview		Asking questions, exploring maternal and infant history including past and present experiences and the meaning of these experiences
Lab Tests		Reviewing laboratory findings
Listen		Listening to sounds
Measure		Determining weight and length of infant, volume of milk expressed, volume of supplements given, etc.
Medical Diagnosis		Medical referral forms or records
Medical History		Reviewing medical records
Observe		Looking, observing visually

Two additional icons are used in the text:

Notice		Clues requiring special follow-up, often referral for medical evaluation
Compensation		Directions for how to think about compensating for this problem

SECTION I
Assessing Breastfeeding

CHAPTER 1

Breastfeeding Dimensions

CHAPTER 2

Optimal Breastfeeding Dynamics

CHAPTER 3

Assessing a Problem Feeding

Breastfeeding Dimensions

1

The physiology of breastfeeding

Breastfeeding integrates both infant and maternal components; feeding at the breast is quite different from most aspects of feeding from a bottle. Successful breastfeeding involves several maternal and infant systems. There are five dimensions to this intricate practice:

- Attachment and suction
- Compression
- Hormonal response of the mother
- Position of the infant
- Compensation

The first dimension: Attachment and suction

Sucking is the primary infant reflex involved in breastfeeding. However, in order to find the breast, the infant uses other senses such as sight, smell, and taste. Once the breast area has been located, the rooting reflex helps the newborn find the mother's nipple. While rooting, the infant turns its head, seeking the nipple, and opens its mouth wide. Once attached to the breast, an infant must be able to suck, swallow, and breathe in synchrony to achieve optimal feeding. Infants cannot be made to develop reflexes; however, occupational therapists have developed some techniques to train the muscles involved, primarily the tongue (Marmet & Shell, 1984; Wolf & Glass, 1992).

The suck reflex begins to develop in early fetal life. In fact, it has been observed as early as 15 to 18 weeks gestation (Wolf & Glass, 1992). At the breast, negative pressure or suction is created by the sealing of the mouth cavity (lips to breast in front, fat pads of the cheeks to breast on the sides, soft palate to tongue in the rear), causing formation of a vacuum that entices milk to flow from a region of higher pressure (the breast) to one of lower pressure (the mouth) when the jaw and tongue drop down to enlarge the oral cavity. This sudden expansion of space creates a vacuum that causes the nipple to elongate about twice its resting length (Smith et al., 1988). The rapid elongation of the nipple, plus the negative pressure of the sealed mouth, draw the milk out of the sinuses.

Types of sucking

- Non-nutritive suck (NNS): Stable lengths of bursts and duration of pauses
- Nutritive suck (NS): A complex pattern that varies over feeding

The length and pattern of bursts (flow) and pauses (no flow) depend on the timing and the size of the let-down (Wolff, 1968).

- Nutritive suck: 1 per second
- Non-nutritive suck: > per second

The second dimension: Compression

Compression, or positive pressure, is created by the closure of the jawbones on the teat, which is formed of the nipple and breast tissue. The infant then uses its tongue, cheek, and jaw muscles to rhythmically massage and compress the teat. The mechanical pressure exerted by the jaws, hard palate, and tongue on the breast forces out the milk stored in the sinus. This is also referred to as "stripping" the breast.

The third dimension: Hormonal response of the mother

In contrast to bottle and cup feeding, breastfeeding is not merely a mechanical function. It is also driven by hormonal responses. The massage-like motions of the infant's hands at the mother's breast, combined with rapid stretching of the nipple in the mouth of the infant, cause a spike in oxytocin levels, which drives the milk ejection reflex (Matthiesen, 2001). Oxytocin release is also affected by conditioned-response triggers—that is, the mother gradually learns to let down her milk in response to environmental cues such as smelling her infant, sitting in her nursing chair, etc. Thus, the flow of milk does not operate by suction, or compression, or hormones alone.

The fourth dimension: Position of the infant

The infant's position and latch affect the removal of maximal amounts of milk from the breast.

Positional attributes
- The angle of the infant's mouth opening
- The infant's lip flare outward
- The distance of the infant's nose and chin from the breast
- The alignment of the infant's head, shoulders, and torso

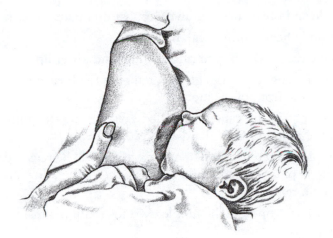

FIGURE 1–1 Well-attached infant.

Used with permission © Health Education Associates

- The relation of level of the infant's mouth to the level of the mother's breast and nipple
- The infant's head tilted slightly backward so that the infant looks up to its mother's face
- The infant's tongue extended, cupping the breast and nipple
- The nipple optimally positioned between the infant's tongue and palate
- The contour of the infant's cheek line rounded and unbroken
- The infant's chin indenting the breast
- The infant's nose close to or touching the breast

Figure 1–1 indicates an infant well-positioned and attached to the breast.

The fifth dimension: Compensation

Anything that gets in the way of the other four dimensions needs to be accounted for, including:

- Maternal and/or infant discomfort
- Supplementation via bottle, cup, or finger
- Congenital anomalies
- Nipple shields and other devices
- Pain for mother and/or infant
- Mother's motivation and other psychosocial aspects
- Infant's temperament/state

Description of functional suckling at the breast

- Licking, tasting, nuzzling
- Gape (wide-open mouth)

- Nipple and breast tissue drawn deeply into infant's mouth
- Lips and cheeks form a seal; lips flange
- Tongue reaches over gum ridge and behind lower lip
- Anterior tongue forms a groove, cupping the breast; peristalsis begins (tongue stays at the front of the mouth)
- Negative pressure caused by sealed cavity draws the nipple (2–3 × length) out past the junction of the hard and soft palate
- If nipple is stretched sufficiently, oxytocin will be released, driving let-down (if nipple is pinched and mother experiences pain, adrenaline may interfere with oxytocin release)
- Lower jaw drops and the nipple expands to fill the inside of the mouth
- Milk flows
- Infant swallows
- Infant breathes
- The suck, swallow, breathe rhythm continues

Optimal Breastfeeding Dynamics

2

Introduction

Like other physiologic processes, it is possible to assess breastfeeding positioning, the latch-on of the infant to the breast, and the transfer of milk from mother to infant. "No assessment, inaccurate assessment, or assessment based on assumption, rather than clinical observation, can result in deleterious outcomes for mothers and infants" (Shrago, 1992).

The importance of correct positioning and the latch-on of the infant to the breast

Optimal breastfeeding is an enjoyable experience for both mother and infant. Sufficient milk is transferred without damage to the breast or nipples. There is no pain. Poor positioning and incorrect latch can lead to sore, painful nipples as well as inadequate milk transfer, which can contribute to the infant's failure to thrive.

In one study, 94% of the mothers who had breastfeeding problems also had incorrect, superficial nipple sucking (Righard, 1998). Only 10% of the mother-infant pairs in the group without breastfeeding problems had incorrect positioning and latch-on. Suboptimal sucking technique (also called "nipple sucking" or "bottle sucking the breast") was much more common among mother-infant pairs with nursing problems of any kind (including infants who are restless between feeds) than among those breastfeeding without problems (94% versus 10%, $P = 0.0001$).

Although faulty breastfeeding technique can be corrected, findings suggest that it is best to encourage optimal technique in the early hours after birth.

The process of optimal breastfeeding includes:

- Observing feeding cues
- Eliciting the gape (wide-open mouth)
- Moving the infant well onto the breast during the gape
- Positioning the lips

- Positioning the nipple
- Forming and maintaining the seal
- Sucking and transferring milk
- Releasing the breast, ending the feed

There are many positions used by breastfeeding dyads. Among those most commonly used are:

- Cradle or madonna position (Figure 2–1). The infant lies on its side, facing mother, with its neck, head, and upper back resting on the mother's forearm next to the breast to be used. Mother may use her opposite hand to support the breast.

- Cross-cradle position (Figure 2–2). The infant lies on its side, facing mother, with its neck, head, and upper back resting in the mother's palm and forearm of the opposite side of the breast being used. Mother may use her other hand to support the breast. This position is especially useful for newborn and preterm infants.

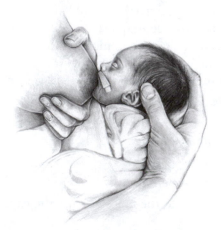

FIGURE 2–3 Football or clutch position.

Used with permission. © Health Education Associates

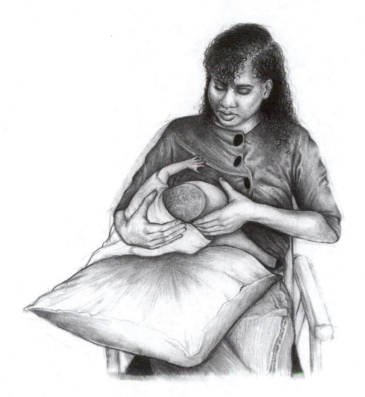

- Football or clutch position (Figure 2–3). The infant lies on its side or back, curled between the side of mother's chest and her arm. The infant's upper body is supported by mother's forearm. The infant's hips are flexed up along the surface that the mother leans against.
- Sidelying position (Figure 2–4). The mother lies on her side. The infant is placed on its side, lying chest-to-chest with mother. Figure 2–5 demonstrates an adaptation of this position to meet the needs of mothers after a Cesarean birth.

FIGURE 2–4 Sidelying position.

Used with permission. © Health Education Associates

Characteristics of optimal breastfeeding

  ### Observing an optimal feeding

A breastfeeding session is optimally observed when the time is right for mother and infant. The environment should be comfortable, with few noises and little movement. It may be difficult to observe an optimal feeding if the mother and infant are uncomfortable and/or not ready to feed. The assessor should first assure the comfort of the mother and the infant. Mother may need help finding a comfortable chair or other location to breastfeed. She may need to be encouraged to make adjustments needed for comfort (e.g., arranging clothing, getting a drink, or making a trip to the bathroom). The infant may need to be changed, undressed before being placed skin-to-skin with the mother, and curled into a comfortable position. Once skin-to-skin, the infant may indicate its readiness to feed and begin feeding with little interruption. Stimuli in the environment may need to be limited (e.g., lights dimmed, noises muted, movement slowed).

 ### Observing for feeding cues and responding to cues by feeding the infant

The breastfeeding session is optimally initiated when the infant exhibits appropriate cues—the infant's signal of readiness to feed. Feeding cues are:

- Rooting—Turning the head, especially with searching movements of the mouth. "The infant actively roots for the breast, turning her head from side to side and opening her mouth wide" (Kitzinger, 1989).

- Increasing alertness.
- Flexing the legs and arms.
- Bringing a hand to the mouth, sucking on a fist or finger.
- Moving the mouth and tongue.
- Crying—Crying is considered a feeding cue but usually does not begin until the other, more subtle cues have failed to elicit the mother's attention. It is more difficult to solve feeding problems when the infant is crying. It is much easier to feed well when those cues that precede crying are used to signal feeding.

Eliciting the gape (wide-open mouth) before attaching to the breast

Gaping occurs when the infant's mouth opens wide (Figure 2–6). "With mouth agape like a hungry cuckoo, the infant comes to breast, his breathing rapid and excited" (Kitzinger, 1989). It is important that mothers not push the nipple into the infant's mouth in the absence of a gape because this is unlikely to result in optimal positioning of the nipple or later appropriate compression of the breast during suckling. Although a variety of lip-tickling techniques have been suggested to encourage the infant to achieve the widest possible mouth opening (such as tickling the infant's lower lip or both lips with the mother's nipple or finger), this should not be necessary for intact infants. Intact infants should gape without lip stimulation if the infant's nose is placed near or touching the nipple, and then the infant is moved a few inches back from the nipple.

The sequence is:

- Place the infant's nose close to the nipple to assist the infant in finding the breast using sight and/or smell.
- Move the infant 1–3 inches away from the nipple.
- Observe the infant gape, opening his or her mouth very wide.
- Repeat the process if the infant fails to gape. If the infant does not attach correctly after the gape, break suction if needed and try again.

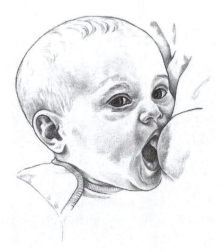

FIGURE 2–6 Infant gapes in approaching breast.

Used with permission. © Health Education Associates

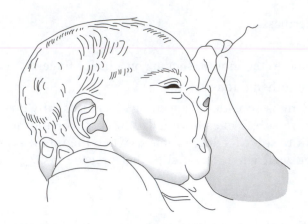

FIGURE 2–7 Infant breastfeeding—note angle of mouth opening.

Used with permission. © Healthy Children 2000 Project

  ## Moving the infant onto the breast during the gape, maintaining a wide-open mouth, and positioning the lips to later compress the milk ducts or sinuses

"At the height of the gape move the infant quickly to the breast, aiming his bottom lip as far away as possible from the base of the nipple" (Mark-It TV, 1996). In optimal gape, the infant attaches to the breast with a wide mouth that has an angle of opening of 140° or more (Figure 2–7). In humans, only the lower jaw can move to accommodate this angle. The infant's head must be able to tilt backwards to achieve this angle, so there must not be excessive pressure against the head from the mother's arm, hand, or from a pillow. The angle of the head tilt must be sufficient to accommodate the dropping of the infant's jaw during suckling. "Move the infant to the breast quick [sic] at the height of the gape, so the chin and lower jaw meet the breast first. The infant feeds with a wide mouth and an active tongue" (Mark-It TV, 1996).

Sufficient areola and breast tissue must be in the infant's mouth in order for the infant to properly milk the breast. The jaw should be positioned over the location of the dilated ducts. It is estimated that the ideal placement of the jaw is 1½–2 inches beyond the base of the nipple. The wide-open gape, optimally placed well onto the breast, will not position the mouth symmetrically around the areola. More of the lower portion of the breast will be in the infant's mouth. Depending on the diameter of the mother's areola, some portion of the areola may be seen at the top of the breast, but be covered at the bottom. The infant's mouth should not be evenly centered around the nipple; it is not like a bull's eye. "You may think that the center of the mouth is halfway between the top and the bottom lip and . . . forget that she has a huge tongue" (Pakkho, 1994).

Positioning the nipple

The nipple should be positioned halfway between the top of the tongue and the roof of the mouth. Optimal position of the mother's nipple inside of the infant's mouth:

- Evokes the secretion of the hormones prolactin and oxytocin,
- Allows for the passage of the maximum milk flow, and
- Places the nipple where it is not abraded during the suckling process.

Ultrasound studies show that the nipple increases in both length and diameter during the feeding (Smith et al., 1988). Optimal suckling requires the nipple to enlarge in order to:

- Contact the roof of the mouth and extend to the soft palate without abrasion.
- Contact the tongue. The tongue's peristalsis forms a bolus, or ball, of milk and moves it to the back of the mouth.
- Contact the inside of the cheeks. Sucking pads will develop inside the cheeks as the infant matures and grows.
- Stretch as the jaw drops allowing maximal mouth opening (Smith et. al., 1988).
- Signal the secretion of prolactin in response to the tactile stimulation of the nipple skin during the nursing.
- Signal the release of oxytocin in response to the stretching of the nipple.
- Deliver the maximum amount of milk rapidly, thereby signaling the milk-making cells to increase production.

The nipple should not be misshapen, abraded, fissured, bruised, or blanched by nursing; any of these may signal incorrect nipple positioning. The infant should be gently removed and repositioned. Color Plate 2–1 demonstrates how the mother may use her finger to break suction. With good attachment, there should be no pain, just a gentle feeling of tugging.

Forming and maintaining the seal with lips, tongue, and breast

The nipple and the breast tissue should remain in the infant's mouth during nursing, although breast movement in concert with the infant's suck may occur. The seal is formed between the infant's lips and tongue and the mother's breast. The seal is supported by the positioning of the infant's head and body.

With correct seal, the:

- Nipple remains in the mouth during suckling.
- Breast tissue is smooth, with no observable wrinkling at the juncture of the mouth and the breast. The mother's breast may move rhythmically as the infant sucks, but remain smooth at the mouth/breast juncture.
- Top and bottom lip are not turned in (Color Plate 2–2). "Lips flanged out and back is a basic part of correct latch" (Minchin, 1989). Incorrect seal occurs when either or both of the lips are turned in.
- Cheek line is smooth, not dimpled or broken. The observation of dimpling in the cheek indicates that there is a positioning problem; the infant's cheeks should not sink inward.
- Tongue is extended. The tongue should be positioned past the gum line of the lower jaw, cupping the breast. The tip of the tongue is visible if the lower lip is pulled back.
- Swallowing of milk is the only sound heard. There is no smacking, clicking, whistling, or noise other than swallowing. (In general, it is rare to hear audible swallows during the colostral phase of lactation.)

Head position and body position align the infant at the breast, stabilizing the head and throat and optimizing the seal. Characteristics of the ideal head and body position of the infant are:

- The infant's nose and chin should be close to the breast. If the chin is away from the breast, the nose is away from the breast, or the nose and chin are both away from the breast, the infant's head is not properly positioned.

- The infant's height at the breast is described as the infant's nose opposite to the mother's nipple before the latch. As the infant's head tilts back for the latch, the nose is no longer at the height opposite the nipple.
- The infant's body should be turned toward the mother's body in a straight line. The infant's head aligns with his or her navel, hips flexed. The infant's arms should not cross over the infant's body. In the early days, the infant's hands knead the breast. This is associated with increased oxytocin secretion, so hands should not be anchored away from the breast.
- The infant's body should be rotated toward the mother. This may be called "tummy-to-tummy" or "chest at the breast" or "chest-to-chest."

Suckling and transferring milk

Sucking occurs when the infant begins to nurse. "Effective infant suckling occurs when as much areola and breast tissue as necessary are drawn into the mouth as he latches on to form an airtight lock around the breast with lips flanged . . . Sucking is unproductive unless there is also swallowing" (Vida Health Communications, 1999).

The infant's nursing dynamic should involve:

- Bursts of two sucks to one swallow, or one suck to one swallow.
- The infant sucks vigorously, stimulating the flow of milk.
- The infant sucks rhythmically. Sucking bursts are separated by pauses and the infant swallows regularly.

Most efficient milk transfer is associated with a:

- Suck-to-swallow ratio of 2:1 and/or 1:1, such as *suck-suck-swallow, suck-suck-swallow, suck-swallow, suck-swallow*. Ratios above 8:1 or *suck-suck-suck-suck-suck-suck-suck-swallow*, are associated with poor milk transfer unless interspersed with 2:1 or 1:1 ratios. Ratios of 5:1 or higher are called "flutter suck" or "non-nutritive suck" and are associated with piston movements of the jaw and poor weight gain in the infant.

Swallow of the milk bolus may be confirmed by auscultation (listening with a stethoscope) of the infant's throat.

Before and after weights of the infant using a precise digital scale will confirm the volume of milk transferred:

- Rocker motion of the infant's jaw extending toward the ear. Ideally, ear movement is seen. Piston or "up and down" motion of the jaw is not associated with efficient milk transfer.

Releasing the breast, ending the feed

Optimal nursing sessions are ended:

- By the infant. This should always be true; only the infant knows when its stomach is full.
- With the infant relaxed. The infant's hands are open, its brow smooth and toes curled, indicating satisfaction. The infant may or may not be asleep, although its eyes are often closed. Mothers describe the look of their satiated infant as "bliss."
- With the mother's nipple unchanged from the shape and color it had at the beginning of the feeding.

- With evidence of sufficient milk transfer: adequate weight gain of ½ pound to 1 pound per week.
- With the mother feeling comfortable and relaxed, no report of pain.

Optimal nursing is *not* defined by:

- Whether the infant nursed on one breast or two.
- How much time passes until the infant next has a feeding cue.
- Whether the infant "sleeps through the night," "sleeps well between feeds," or "goes several hours in between feedings." Sleepy infants are usually a warning sign, not a sign of satisfaction. Calorically deprived infants are sleepy and apathetic feeders.
- Whether or not the infant is "good." So-called "good" infants may not have sufficient energy to draw the mother's attention.

Assessing a Problem Feeding

3

Introduction

One of the difficulties of assessing the dynamics of breastfeeding is that the assessor must rely on the outside appearance of an intricate, internal choreography of reflexes: suck-swallow-breathe on the part of the infant, and manufacture and ejection of milk on the mother's part. Few tools exist for visualizing the interior workings of breastfeeding. Ultrasound and x-ray studies have been done of infants presenting with severe feeding difficulty; however, these tools are not accessible to many assessors. Most assessors rely on a range of visual and auditory clues to identify and improve feeding difficulties. It is important to recognize that the presence of clues is not necessarily problematic. In fact, one of the most difficult challenges for the novice breastfeeding assessor is to refrain from correcting the obvious "less than ideal" components of the feeding techniques of nursing couplets. The only components that need improvement are those that result in:

- Pain for the mother
- Discomfort for the infant
- Inadequate milk production and flow

Many thriving, happy nursing dyads have unusual or uncomfortable-looking feeding postures. However, the mother and infant should be left alone unless problems are present.

The infant should be observed for readiness before attempting feeding assessment. It is unlikely that appropriate feeding will be observed if the mother and infant are not ready to feed.

Gape

It is expected that the infant will open its mouth wide when brought within range of the nipple. Variations on the wide-open gape associated with feeding problems are explained in the following section.

No gape

Lack of a gape reflex is of concern and needs to be further evaluated. A consistent lack of gape should be referred for pediatric work-up. Related conditions include:

- Prematurity
- Congenital condition (neurologic or muscular impairment)
- Malnutrition
- Dehydration

    **Narrow gape**

Color Plate 3–1 shows a gape of 90° or less, which is associated with nipple soreness and inadequate milk transfer. The infant may exhibit a narrow gape for a variety of reasons, including:

- Inappropriate timing of feeding (e.g., attempting to feed the infant when infant is not hungry).
- Lack of coordination of feeding between mother and infant (e.g., mother attempting to force the feeding or the feeding position).
- Poor positioning (e.g., infant's head too far forward to fully drop lower jaw to achieve wide-open gape).
- Tight mouth. Infants who have experienced invasive and/or painful oral procedures may become orally aversive and protect their mouths by clamping the jaw or pursing the lips. Examples of such procedures include deep or vigorous suctioning, rough oral examinations, and gavage tube placements.

- Receding chin, unable to touch breast. Congenital conditions such as micrognathia (abnormal smallness of the jaw), Pierre Robin syndrome (micrognathia combined with cleft palate, downward placement of the tongue, and absent gag reflex), and other malformations of the lower jaw may limit the ability of the infant to feed well. Color Plate 3–2 shows a lateral view of an infant with a very receding chin (mandible). The poor juxtaposition of mandible and maxilla causes breastfeeding problems. Infant is supine and yawning.

 Changes to positioning of the infant with these conditions may increase milk transfer. Positions that put the infant in an upright, vertical position may increase amount of breast grasped.

 When the infant's chin does not, or is unable to, touch the breast during a feeding, grasp of the breast and, thus, potential transfer of milk, is limited.

 - Chin tucked.
When the infant's head is too far forward, maximal jaw opening is limited because of compression of the jaw against the chest.

 If the head is freed up and allowed to move back, more optimal jaw opening can be achieved.

 - Nose blocked by breast.
Improper position can cause the infant's nostrils to be blocked. The infant will be unable to feed effectively because of the need to break suction in order to breathe.

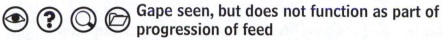 **Gape seen, but does not function as part of progression of feed**

The infant opens its mouth and is seen to root and gape, but does not seem to sense the presence of the nipple and breast in its mouth, and does not latch on. This may be related to:

- Overly full or edematous breast
- Short, flat, or inverted nipple
- Prematurity
- Neuromuscular difficulties

   Seal

To trigger the rapid expansion of the nipple in the infant's mouth and, thus, the flow of milk, the infant must create a seal at the breast with its lips, mouth, and throat. Variations on the ability to form a seal at the breast include:

  Unable to form a seal

- Cleft lip. This congenital defect is a separation of the upper lip. Clefts can occur on one side (unilateral) or both sides (bilateral). The infant shown in Color Plate 3–3 has a unilateral cleft lip and cleft palate.

 Depending on the extent of the cleft and the fullness and the flexibility of the mother's breast tissue, the cleft may be closed by angling the infant at the breast in such a way that the cleft is filled with breast tissue. Some mothers have been successful at using their thumb to close the cleft and create the seal necessary for successful feeding.

- Cleft palate. The presence of this opening in the roof of the mouth makes it difficult for the infant to attain a true seal at the breast. Color Plate 3–4 offers an interior view of the unilateral cleft.

 Some mothers are successful at using angled latch-on to fill a unilateral cleft. A palatal obturator—a dental plate made to cover the cleft—has been used to enhance breastfeeding for some cleft palate infants.

- Choanal atresia. The infant with this congenital opening between the nasal cavity and the pharynx may have difficulty sustaining a seal at the breast.

 Infants with craniofacial anomalies need intensive follow-up with frequent weight checks.

     Able to form a seal, but difficulty maintaining the seal

If the infant is able to form a seal, but has difficulty maintaining the seal and holding the nipple in his or her mouth, it may be related to the following situations:

- Poor positioning. Awkward positioning at the breast can make it difficult for the infant to maintain a seal, particularly when the infant's head is turned toward the shoulder.
- Congenital anomalies, such as cardiac, respiratory, or neuromuscular, in the infant.

- Prematurity.
- Palatal anomalies. In addition to clefts of the palate, infants with unusually high or misshapen palates may have difficulty maintaining a seal at the breast (Marmet & Shell, 1993). Intubation of a premature or ill infant may result in a grooved palate (Wilson-Clay & Hoover, 1999).
- Jaundice. The infant experiencing hyperbilirubinemia "may be depressed and lethargic and therefore may not nurse well" (Lawrence & Lawrence, 1999).

 Visible jaundice, or yellowing of the skin, requires medical evaluation.

- Dehydration/malnutrition. Poorly hydrated and/or poorly nourished infants may have difficulty sustaining the energy required to maintain seal and suckle at the breast.

 Tongue

The tongue plays a major role in feeding. The tongue draws in nipple and breast tissue to form a teat. It also seals off the back of the mouth cavity and forms a central groove that stabilizes the teat, forms the ball or bolus of milk, and moves the bolus toward the back of the mouth where it is swallowed (Wolf & Glass, 1992).

Feeding problems associated with the tongue include:

- Inability to extend the tongue beyond the alveolar gum ridge. This may be due to congenital anomaly, such as short tongue and ankyloglossia (abnormal shortness of the frenulum or membrane under the tongue). Ankyloglossia is also known as tight lingual frenulum, or "tongue-tie." This anomaly, shown in Color Plate 3–5, is associated with painful latch-on and nipples in the mother and potential poor milk transfer and weight gain in the infant. Infants with ankyloglossia may be able to nurse well, or may have difficulty.

 These infants may be better able to nurse in a very deeply latched position.

 Infants who are unable to elicit good milk flow should be referred to a physician for evaluation of the frenulum.

- Difficulty forming a groove with the tongue. This may be associated with neurological and/or muscular impairment.
- Hypertonicity. High oral muscle tone in the infant is associated with several appearances of the tongue:
  - Elevated tongue tip
  - Humped tongue (tongue is compressed from front to back)
  - Bunched tongue (tongue is compressed from side-to-side)
  - Tongue thrusting (forceful expulsion of the tongue during feeding)
- Hypotonicity. Low muscle tone is associated with tongue protrusion (tongue often protrudes between lips at rest as well as during feedings). In an effort to maintain head and neck position, the infant with low tone may also tense the muscles of the mouth, resulting in elevated tongue tip and tongue retraction (Wolf & Glass, 1992).

 **Lip**

Ideally, the lips flare out to form the outward seal to breast tissue. When the infant is not positioned properly, the lips may not flare and seal correctly. Other feeding problems associated with the lips include:

- Cleft lip (see "Seal").
- Limitation of the ability to flare the upper lip may be caused by tight labial frenulum (the membrane attaching the upper lip to the gum).

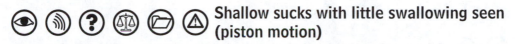 **Milk transfer**

Many factors affect an infant's ability to transfer an adequate amount of milk during a feeding. The following are hallmarks of possible milk transfer problems. However, many well-nourished infants exhibit the same type of activity without associated problems with milk supply.

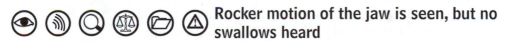 **Shallow sucks with little swallowing seen (piston motion)**

Shallow sucking is associated with limited milk transfer and little swallowing. A piston-like motion of the chin moving rapidly up and down in a biting-like action is often seen with shallow sucking, as shown in Figure 3–1. If the assessor observes only piston motion of the jaw during a feeding, this may be related to:

- Prematurity. This may influence the infant's physiologic ability and energy level.
- Poor positioning. This impacts the depth of latch, limiting the amount of breast tissue compressed, thus limiting the potential for milk transfer.
- Malnutrition and dehydration. Infants with these problems may be unable to sustain active feeding for a long period of time.

Rocker motion of the jaw is seen, but no swallows heard

A rocker motion of the jaw describes the motion of the jaw swinging forward from the hinge beneath the ear, rocking the jaw forward to indent the breast, as is indi-

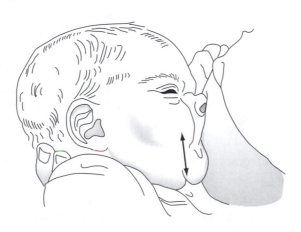

FIGURE 3–1   Piston-like motion.

Used with permission. © Healthy Children 2000 Project

FIGURE 3–2 Rocker
motion.

*Used with permission. © Healthy
Children 2000 Project*

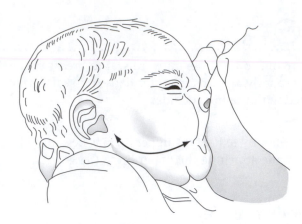

cated in Figure 3–2. The presence of rocker motion without audible swallowing may
indicate:

- Poor positioning and/or latch
- Lack of milk to transfer—low milk supply

Misshapen nipple at the end of a feeding

The appearance of the nipple when the infant detaches from the breast can assist in
detecting improper attachment. The nipple should come out of the infant's mouth
as an everted, tubular shape, markedly longer than its resting position, but otherwise normal in appearance. When suboptimal breastfeeding occurs, the nipple may
appear to be pinched and may bear white lines or spots, or be otherwise misshapen
immediately after the feeding ends. Color Plate 3–6 shows an angled/beveled nipple
just after breastfeeding. This indicates a sucking, latch, or positioning problem.

Assessing milk sufficiency

Concerns about inadequate milk supply are extremely common among breastfeeding women. In fact, "not enough milk" is the most common reason women give for
early cessation of breastfeeding. It is widely acknowledged that fears about milk inadequacy may reflect either a real problem or a perceived problem. An adequate milk
supply is crucial for infant growth. It is therefore imperative to carefully assess any
concerns that the mother may have about milk supply and to distinguish between
true milk insufficiency and perceived inadequacy. The following are methods for assessing the volume of milk transferred:

- Visual cues. The well-nourished infant eagerly seeks the breast, latches on, and
  feeds vigorously with rocker motion of the jaw. As the infant nurses and receives
  milk, its body tone will soften, its hands will open, and its head will fall back
  slightly. Under the influence of oxytocin, the mother's body tone also softens and
  she seems more relaxed.

- Auditory clues. When there is an adequate milk supply, swallowing will be heard
  during the feeding.

- Weight gain. The infant will gain weight appropriately, increasing ½ to 1 pound
  of body weight in each of the early weeks. When available, the use of a precise
  digital scale with breastmilk intake function, as seen in Color Plate 3–7, can help

to document the volume of milk transfer during a feed. Many experienced assessors have been surprised to learn that little or no milk was transferred during a nursing that had all the hallmarks of an optimal feeding. Likewise, some passively nursing infants transfer a large amount of milk. Use of pre- and post-feed weights provide objective data to quantify milk transfer.

- Infant output measures. The infant should pass meconium (tarry, black stool) within the first 24 hours of life. By the fifth day, the infant should have three or four breastmilk stools (mustard yellow and seedy) and at least six urinations daily (American Academy of Pediatrics [AAP], 1997).

Color

Maintenance of color, heart rate, and oxygenation at the breast is characteristic of the mature, healthy infant. Inability to maintain these markers of infant physiologic stability during feeding may reflect:

- Prematurity
- Congenital anomaly, especially cardiac
- Illness such as sepsis
- Exposure to medications and other drugs

Assessing a breastfeeding

Wolf and Glass (1992) suggest a five-step assessment/evaluation process:

1. Gather information and plan for the visit. Review any pertinent information prior to interviewing the mother and infant. This includes review of any information or documentation available concerning this mother and infant (e.g., the mother's and/or infant's chart, notes from telephone conversations, notes from referral source, etc.). Planning includes assembling any items and equipment that are expected to be used during the assessment (e.g., comfortable chair for mother, infant scale, etc.).

2. Feeding observation entails three portions:
    - General observation: The assessor's observations regarding the physiologic status of and general interaction between the mother and infant.
    - Naturalistic observation: Observation of a portion of a usual breastfeeding interchange between mother and infant. This is best performed without intervention from the assessor.
    - Elicited observation: Observation of the outcome of assessor-suggested modification of aspects of a feeding (e.g., changes to position, attachment, etc.).

3. Exploration of strategies for improvement:
    - The development of hypotheses for improving the feeding interaction based on history and observed phenomena.
    - Discussion with mother of hypotheses generated, including pros and cons of various methods for improving the feeding outcome.
    - Testing of agreed strategies.

4. Synthesis of a plan:

    ○ All observed data, hypotheses, and strategies are synthesized into an action plan for feeding management that is agreed upon between the assessor and the mother.

5. Communication of results:

    ○ Reiterate findings and action plans for the mother. The language used to describe the situation is extremely important. The assessor should take great care to avoid terminology that blames, negatively characterizes, or labels the mother or infant. Review plans with the mother to assure that the plan is achievable and agreeable to all parties.

    ○ Document the outcomes of the assessment and evaluation.

    ○ Communicate findings to key healthcare providers in accordance with mother's consent to release information. Clearly identify and refer any items that need further medical evaluation.

SECTION II

Assessing the Infant

CHAPTER 4

Optimal Breastfeeding: The Infant's Role

CHAPTER 5

Behavioral Assessment of the Infant in Relation to Suboptimal Breastfeeding

Optimal Breastfeeding: The Infant's Role

4

Introduction

Infants born at or around term should be active participants in the budding breast-feeding relationship. Immediately after birth, the healthy newborn (condition permitting) should be placed skin-to-skin with the mother. The infant will use stepping and crawling behaviors to move to the breast, find the nipple, attach, and begin suckling, as shown in Figure 4–1. Newborn infants are capable of locating the nipple (probably because of the location of the mother's heartbeat and the fact that the secretions of the Montgomery glands smell similar to the familiar amniotic fluid), grasping the nipple, shaping it, and sucking. All healthy infants are awake, alert, and capable of initiating breastfeeding in the first hour after birth. For many infants, this period of alertness continues into the second hour after birth.

For later feedings, the infant signals the mother that it is time to feed. During the feeding, the infant's grasping, stretching, and stroking of the nipple stimulates the hormones that make and deliver milk. In addition, the infant transfers the milk from the breast to his or her mouth, forms the milk into a bolus, and swallows.

Active, integrated infants who are mature and coordinated still require the mother to be behaviorally and physiologically responsive in order to be optimally fed.

FIGURE 4–1 Infant crawling up to the breast.

Used with permission. © Health Education Associates

Gestational age and size

Infants are classified by gestational age and size. An infant's gestational age is helpful in determining general capabilities and expectations. All infants are individuals, however, and individual capabilities must be taken into account.

Gestational age

Assessment of gestational age determines approximate infant age since conception, so the assessment may be done during pregnancy or after the infant is born. Assessment of gestational age helps in understanding:

- Appropriateness of other findings
- Possible morbidities that are more common at various gestational ages
- Infant's risk of death

  Prenatal determination of gestational age may be based on calculations using:
- Date of the mother's last menstrual period
- Date of the first reported fetal activity (quickening usually occurs at around 16–18 weeks)
- Date of first reported fetal heart sounds (usually 10–12 weeks, determined by Doppler examination)
- Ultrasound examination (before 20 weeks)

  After the infant is born, gestational age is determined by physical and neurologic criteria, usually using The New Ballard Score (Ballard et al., 1991) or the Dubowitz assessment tool (Dubowitz et al., 1970).

  Infants are classified by gestational age into three broad categories:

- Preterm: < 37 weeks gestation
- Term: ≥ 37 to < 42 weeks gestation
- Post-term: ≥ 42 weeks gestation

Gestational size

Infants are also classified by size; that is, the amount of growth in utero:

- Small for gestational age (SGA): The infant's birth weight is <10th percentile for gestational age.
- Appropriate for gestational age (AGA): The infant's birth weight is between the 10th and 90th percentile for gestational age.
- Large for gestational age (LGA): The infant's birth weight is >90th percentile for gestational age.
- Infants with birth weight under 2,500 grams are considered low birth weight (LBW).
- Infants with a birth weight under 1,500 grams are considered very low birth weight (VLBW).
- Infants with a birth weight at or under 800 grams are considered extremely low birth weight (ELBW).

Coordinated suck-swallow-breathe

Both breast- and bottle-feeding require the infant to coordinate his or her sucking, swallowing, and breathing reflexes. In general, the ability to coordinate sucking, swallowing, and breathing at birth correlates with the maturity of the infant. Premature infants should be assessed for the ability to coordinate the suck, swallow, breathe activity and have a functioning gag reflex before nursing at the breast. Oxygenation is better maintained during breastfeeding than during bottlefeeding, and there are fewer episodes of apnea while breastfeeding than when the same infant feeds from a bottle.

The sucking reflex is usually present at 32–34 weeks of gestation, although many infants do not develop a coordinated suck-swallow until 37 weeks gestation. The gag reflex is normally present at birth. This protective reflex contracts the muscles of the soft palate in response to stimulation of the back of the tongue and soft palate. During breastfeeding, the nipple and a portion of the breast are drawn into the infant's mouth. The breast and nipple tissue forms a teat that completely fills the infant's open mouth. The nipple tip is drawn way back into the mouth while the tongue cups and compresses the breast and nipple tissue. This sucking action is coordinated with the infant's breathing and swallowing.

  ## Infant state

Infants move between six states of wakefulness, sleeping, and crying:

Deep sleep

During the state of deep sleep (Figure 4–2), the infant exhibits no body movements, no rapid eye movement (REM, or fluttering of the eyeball visible under the eyelid), and breathing is quiet and regular. When infants are in the deep sleep state, they cannot be easily aroused and will feed poorly, if at all. Infants spend only 20–30 minutes in deep sleep before moving to light/active sleep.

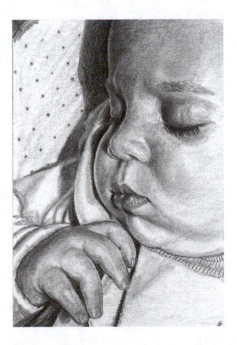

FIGURE 4–2   Deep sleep state.

Used with permission. © Health Education Associates

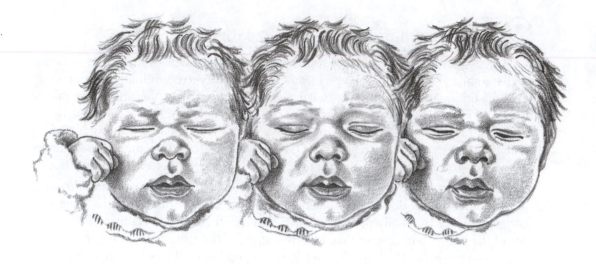

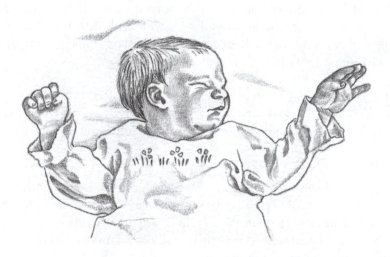

Light sleep or active sleep

During the state of light sleep (Figure 4–3), the infant exhibits REM, body movements, irregular breathing patterns, and sporadic sucking movements. Infants spend most of their sleep time in this kind of sleep. The infant can move from light/active sleep to drowsy and quiet alert or into deeper sleep. When REM is seen, the infant can be brought to the breast and will usually feed well—even without opening its eyes or becoming more awake.

Drowsy

During the drowsy state (Figure 4–4), the infant may open and close its eyes, have increased body movements such as yawning and stretching, and make little sounds. Infants brought to the breast while in this state will usually feed well. The infant may become more alert and bright-eyed during the feeding.

Quiet alert

During the quiet alert state (Figure 4–5), the infant is interactive and responsive. The infant looks around, is bright-eyed, has smooth body movements, and even, regular breaths. Although this state is often recommended as the best for breast-

FIGURE 4–5   Quiet alert state.

Used with permission. © Health Education Associates

feeding, some infants may move too quickly from quiet alert into active alert and crying states before the feed begins. This may result in feeding problems.

Active alert

During the active alert state (Figure 4–6), the infant increases arm and leg movements, perhaps waving the limbs around. The infant may become fussy and move into the crying state or may move into the quiet alert state.

FIGURE 4–6   Active alert state.

Used with permission. © Health Education Associates

FIGURE 4–7 Crying state.

*Used with permission. © Health
Education Associates*

Crying

During the crying state (Figure 4–7), the young infant needs a comforting adult to aid in moving into a more organized state. A crying infant is difficult to orient to the breast for a feeding. Moving the infant to a more organized state prior to the feeding attempt will enhance the success of the feeding.

Approach and avoidance signals

In addition to noting the infant's state, observing the infant's behaviors can indicate whether the infant is willing to be approached (approach behaviors) or if the infant needs help to become more organized (avoidance behaviors).

Feeding cues are specific approach behaviors

Approach behaviors signal the infant's desire for interaction on many levels. Feeding cues illustrate a specific approach behavior requesting nourishment:

- Mouthing and sucking. The mouth, lips, and jaws move in a searching or sucking motion. The mouthing behavior may be organized into sucks that can be directed to its own hands and fingers, the mother's fingers, or other objects. Sucking may occur in a searching motion involving head movements.
- Subtle body movements, wiggling.
- REM, or rapid eye movement, under the infant's closed eyelid.
- Rooting or turning toward a cheek that is stroked or touched.
- Moving hand to mouth, moving hands to the head and face.

Energy

Breastfeeding uses less energy than does feeding from a bottle, even if the infant is premature. However, breastfeeding does require the infant to be interactive. Infants who are well nourished feed best. Infants who do not have sufficient energy to feed become weaker, more apathetic, and may fail to thrive. Unfortunately, popular

👁 📶	Common approach behaviors in infants	Common avoidance behaviors in infants (See Color Plate 4–1)
Face and mouth activities	• The infant's tongue repeatedly extends and relaxes.	• The infant spits up more than a passive drool, gags, or has nonsynchronized swallowing and breathing patterns.
	• The infant rounds its mouth and purses its lips.	• The infant grunts, indicating a bowel movement, retracts the lips, or grimaces.
Hand and arm activities	• The infant moves its hands onto its face or ears and holds them in place.	• The infant splays its fingers, extending its fingers with the fingers separated from each other.
	• The infant holds onto its mother's hand or finger.	• The infant fully extends its arms into the air together or singly.
	• The infant grasps its own hands or clutches its hands to the body.	
Leg and feet activities	• The infant folds its legs in a crossed position or places its feet sole to sole.	• The infant extends its legs into midair, either one at a time or together.
Body activities	• The infant curls its trunk, flexes its hips, and tucks its arms.	• The infant "airplanes" by extending the arms out to the side at shoulder level, the upper and lower arms may be at an angle to each other.
		• The infant may startle.
Visual activities	• The infant locks onto a person's face or other object and maintains a gaze.	• The infant actively averts its eyes, perhaps momentarily closing them.

Adapted from University of New York, Stony Brook, 1994.

thinking may lead parents to believe that an infant who sleeps several hours, feeds briefly, and sleeps again is a normal feeding pattern. An infant who meets this description is actually an infant who needs to consume more calories in order to feed actively, more efficiently, and more frequently.

Energy characteristics of normal term infants

- Normal heart rate is 100–180 beats per minute, usually 120–160 beats per minute when awake.
- Normal respiratory rate in the newborn is 30–60 breaths per minute.
- Heart and respiratory rates remain stable during breastfeeding.

Neuromuscular system

Several aspects of the neuromuscular system are involved in feeding. Major nerves that make feeding possible include all 12 cranial nerves.

Infant musculature involved in breastfeeding includes (Walker, 2002):

- Muscles of chewing and swallowing: temporalis, masseter, medial pterygoid, lateral pterygoid, buccinator, and obricularis oris

- Muscles moving the tongue: genioglossus, styloglossus, stylohyoid, digastric, mylohyoid, hyoglossus, and geniohyoid
- Muscles moving the throat: sternohyoid, omohyoid, sternothyroid, and thyrohyoid

The intact infant has a functional neurologic and muscular system to assist in feeding at the breast, including:

- Rhythmic sucking
- Ability to place body in flexion at elbows, knees, and ankles, as shown in Color Plate 4–2
- Appropriate reaction to stimulation
- Ability to orient to the breast, concentrate and work at feeding
- Capability of becoming more organized when soothed
- Intact suck reflex, gag reflex, and rooting reflex
- Ability to coordinate the suck, swallow, breathe pattern

The normal newborn is expected to breastfeed 8–12 times or more per 24 hours (AAP, 1997).

Normal characteristics of term infants

When the infant is observed unswaddled and without contact in a quiet awake or light sleep state, the infant has:

- Moderate flexion of all four limbs
- Symmetry from side to side, including the face
- Motor activity appropriate for the physiological state
- Smooth, spontaneous movements
- An expressive face with yawning or crying
- A loud, lusty cry

Desire

Ideally, the infant approaches the breast and works actively to achieve feeding. Infants are capable of long periods of concentration. If the infant is in the active alert, quiet alert, or drowsy state, it will work toward achieving the feeding especially if the feeding attempt is preceded by skin-to-skin contact with the mother's chest.

Orientation

Within minutes after birth, intact infants are able to orient to the breast and nipple to initiate feeding. Some infants need more time, but most are capable of feeding within the first 2 hours. Skin-to-skin contact provides a favorable beginning to breastfeeding and allows the infant an opportunity to familiarize to the breast, hear its mother's heartbeat, smell the Montogomery gland secretions, and then begin to lick and suckle.

Coordination

Suck, swallow, and breathe are coordinated in the intact infant born after 37 weeks of gestation and may be coordinated as early as 32 weeks of gestation.

 Muscle tone

Appropriate facial muscle tone is needed for the lips to form a seal at the breast, drop the jaw, and produce a strong suck. The muscular tongue cups the mother's nipple and breast tissue. Peristalsis of the tongue forms the milk into a bolus and moves it to the back of the mouth.

 Gape

The wide-open gape occurs when the infant is moved away from breast after smelling, licking, or touching the nipple. It is expected that the infant's mouth will open as wide during the gape as during a yawn. Gape is maximized when the head is tilted back so that the infant looks up at the mother's face.

 Profile

When the infant is breastfeeding, its profile should show the chin indenting the breast. The nose may touch the breast or be very close, assuring that the infant has room to breathe. In order for the jaw to drop maximally, the infant's head should be supported but not pushed toward the breast. This can be achieved by the mother placing a supporting hand at the nape of the infant's neck and at the shoulders, rather than on the back of the head.

  Seal

The infant forms a teat with the indrawn nipple and breast tissue. The infant creates and holds a seal with the lips and tongue so that the nipple remains in place during many minutes of suck-swallow-breathe action. The tongue should extend beyond the lower gum line, aiding the seal. Although the sound of swallowing may be noisy, clicking sounds are not associated with maintenance of the seal. Breast tissue is smooth at the junction of the lips and the breast.

   Milk transfer

It is expected that breastfeeding infants will gain ½ to 1 ounce per day in the early weeks. Adequate weight gain is an excellent indication of milk transfer. Assessment of milk transfer at a single feed should include:

- Suck: Swallow ratio of 2:1, or 1:1 is seen and heard in a repeating pattern during the feeding.
- Rocker motion of the lower jaw is noted, including ear movement during the deep sucks.
- Cheeks are rounded with no dimples. No smacking or clicking sounds are heard.
- Before and after weights using a digital scale can be used to indicate the amount of the milk transfer.

Infant output

Infant urinary and stool output is also a good measure of milk intake. It is expected that the normal breastfed infant will:

- Pass meconium (tarry black newborn stools) within the first 24 hours of life (Lawrence & Lawrence, 1999) (Color Plate 4–3).

- Pass transitional stools (black transitioning to green, then brownish yellow) within the first days of life. Color Plate 4–4 shows transitional stool of a 4-day-old breastfed baby, with both meconium and breastmilk stool in one diaper.

- Have three or four normal stools daily by 5–7 days of age (AAP, 1997). Stools of the adequately breastfed infant are yellow, seedy, and occur frequently, often during or after every feeding. Color Plate 4–5 indicates normal breastmilk stool in diaper.

- Urinate at least six times per day (AAP, 1997).

 Color

During the feed, the infant's color is maintained, oxygen saturation remains normal, and the heart rate is stable. The infant's energy level remains sufficient to achieve completion of the feeding.

 Response

The infant appears comfortable at breast, relaxes during the feeding, detaches spontaneously, and appears satiated or full. The infant may want to feed again in only a few minutes. The mother should continue to watch for feeding cues and nurse the infant on cue.

Signs of satiety include:

- Relaxed infant body posture, hands relaxed, toes curled
- "Milk drunk" expression; the infant smiles and rolls its head in a delightful way

Behavioral Assessment of the Infant in Relation to Suboptimal Breastfeeding

5

Introduction

If breastfeeding is not progressing optimally, the infant is at risk for malnutrition, dehydration, and other untoward consequences. Assessment of the infant should include skills required for breastfeeding, including the infant's:

- State, especially the infant's ability to move smoothly from one state to another
- Energy, especially the infant's ability to interact and sustain a feeding
- Response to the feeding activity
- Performance related to neuromuscular capacity and ability
- Cueing related to signaling readiness to feed
- Desire or interest in the feeding
- Orientation to the breast, nipple, and feeding
- Coordination of the skills related to feeding

Assessment of infant state

Assessment of the infant's behavior is accomplished primarily through observation. An infant may make frequent transitions between states. Full-term infants are expected to do this smoothly.

 Preterm, neurologically impaired, or underfed infants change abruptly between sleep and wake states.

Maintaining or creating an organized state

- The infant must be able to self-organize to breastfeed effectively. When interacting with the environment (the mother, the breast, suckling, diaper changing), a disorganized infant is *unable* to:
  - Console itself (usually achieved with hand-to-mouth movements)
  - Be consoled easily (when held and soothed, for example)

 If the infant cannot console him- or herself, a plan is required that seeks to assist the infant. Plans might include swaddling the infant and reducing stimuli.

The disorganized infant will react to stimuli with:

- Frantic movements
- Jittery movements
- Color changes
- Irregular respiration
- Hypotonia; neurologically impaired infants generally have low muscle tone not only in reaction to stimuli

 Talking, feeding, or caring for an infant with a low tolerance for stimuli may cause stress or fatigue; limitation of stimuli may improve feeding.

- The premature or ill infant is less likely to be able to maintain a state of organization

 Inability to maintain or regain a state of organization in an otherwise intact and seemingly mature infant may indicate impeding illness or an ominous physiologic change and should be evaluated promptly.

Infants who are excessively lethargic or extremely irritable should be referred for immediate medical evaluation.

Breastfeeding and the sleep states

Books for parents and health-care providers describe infants as sleeping as many as 22 hours a day. Parents may believe that sleeping infants should not be disturbed and, as a result, may begin a cycle of inadequate feedings and lowered maternal milk supply. Although deep sleep is not an ideal state for breastfeeding, light or active sleep may be. Figure 5–1 shows a feeding cue that many parents may miss.

 Infants in deep sleep should transition easily to light or active sleep, although the arousal may be brief before returning to deep sleep.

The majority of a newborn infant's sleep is in light or active sleep stages. Preterm infants spend more time in this state than do full-term infants. Full-term infants spend more time in the deep sleep and alert states.

Drowsiness is a transitional state in which the infant's eyes are heavily lidded, although they open and close. Although the infant's response to stimuli is delayed, he or she may be encouraged through gentle stimuli to move into an alert state or, through soothing, to move back to a deeper sleep state. Infants may stretch, yawn, startle, and make little sounds in the drowsy state.

 Offering an infant the breast during the light sleep or drowsy stages is an effective strategy for dealing with the infant who has a very quick transition from the deep sleep to active alert stages.

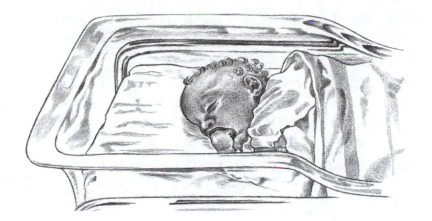

FIGURE 5–1 Infant demonstrates a feeding cue— sucking on its fist.

Used with permission. © Health Education Associates

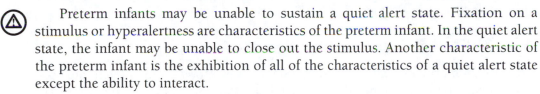 Breastfeeding and the alert states

Quiet alert is the most interactive state for the infant. Full-term newborns have their first quiet alert state for the first 2 hours or so after birth. This is an ideal time to initiate skin-to-skin contact and for the infant to learn about breastfeeding.

Preterm infants may be unable to sustain a quiet alert state. Fixation on a stimulus or hyperalertness are characteristics of the preterm infant. In the quiet alert state, the infant may be unable to close out the stimulus. Another characteristic of the preterm infant is the exhibition of all of the characteristics of a quiet alert state except the ability to interact.

Infants in the quiet alert state will work continuously toward the goal of feeding. The mother who waits for crying as the cue to feed may have an infant who becomes easily frustrated and disorganized. Skin-to-skin contact, swaddling, decreasing environmental stimulation, and rocking, may calm the infant and allow a transition to quiet alert.

Active alert is characterized by increasing movements and increased sensitivity to stimuli. The infant does not pay attention in the same bright-eyed way that he or she does in the quiet alert state. Periods of fussiness and rapid or irregular breathing also characterize the active alert state.

The intact mature infant is able to be consoled during times of fussiness or may console itself. Preterm, ill, or impaired infants may be unable to self-console or respond to the soothing activities of the mother. An otherwise undiagnosed infant who is noted to be chronically or suddenly inconsolable requires prompt evaluation.

Crying is characterized by increased motor activity, color changes, and exaggerated response to unpleasant stimuli. Crying infants may console themselves by returning to a lower state. Signs of stress in a crying infant include apnea, vomiting, and a decrease in oxygen saturation.

Preterm, ill, or impaired infants may have a very weak (or absent) cry. A chronically or suddenly weak cry should signal prompt, further evaluation.

Crying is a normal state for infants, but prolonged or inconsolable crying may be indicative of illness or a medical emergency. Further evaluation may be needed.

Crying that is defined as colic-like has the following characteristics:

- The infant is inconsolable.
- The infant cries without reasonable cause.
- The infant cries for more than 3 hours a day.

To qualify as colic-like crying, the behavior must happen at least 3 days a week for at least 3 weeks (Wessel, 1954).

Assessment of an infant's energy to feed

Adequate intake of nourishment for energy is imperative for infants. Among other reasons, infants need sufficient energy to:

- Grow
- Develop
- Feed

A common misconception is that poorly feeding infants can be "starved" into becoming better feeders. Although breastfeeding requires less energy than does feeding from a bottle, infants who are calorically deprived become more and more apathetic at feeding. While the infant should be followed on a growth chart by a pediatrician, a rough guideline is that the infant should gain ½ pound to 1 pound per week in the early weeks.

   Lethargy or apathy related to feeding

Lethargy is abnormal in intact, full-term infants. It is important to differentiate possible reasons for lethargic or apathetic feeding before planning feeding strategies. The assessor must also clearly understand the reasons for the onset of apathy. Lethargic feeders:

- Fall asleep at the breast without transferring sufficient milk
- Exhibit few feeding cues
- Sleep more than 2–3 hours consistently between feedings

  Consider whether the infant:

- Always feeds lethargically or feeds well under any particular conditions (upright, lying down, during the day, at night, in one position or the other).
- Is jaundiced. See the yellow appearance of the infant's skin shown in Color Plate 5–1. Infants with high bilirubin levels appear very sleepy and may be unable to sustain energy for feeding.

 Visibly jaundiced infants should be referred for medical evaluation.

- Fed well at first but has become more apathetic as the days and hours have passed.
- Has been exposed to drugs (e.g., labor and medication drugs, prescription or over-the-counter medications, illegal drugs) that may pass through the milk from the mother to the infant, resulting in lethargy or drowsiness.
- Is immature, with insufficient energy for feeding especially for many minutes.
- Has a congenital condition that requires more energy than the infant has been able to take in.

- Is malnourished due to previous poor feedings. In a failure-to-thrive infant, Vitamin D or zinc deficiency may be related to poor growth.

- Is dehydrated (may be due to poor feeding, diarrhea, or other illness or condition). Symptoms of dehydration include:

  ○ Weight loss of more than 7% of birth weight

  ○ Dry skin and mucous membranes with poor turgor, such as the infant shown in Color Plate 5–2

  ○ Weak cry

  ○ Lethargy

  ○ Scant urinary output (urine may also be concentrated) with few or no stools, including a prolonged duration of meconium if in the immediate week or 2 postpartum

  ○ Apathetic feeding at the breast, including falling asleep during the feeding, sleeping more than 2–3 hours between feeds, and being difficult to awaken

  ○ Depressed fontanels, which may be a late and ominous sign of dehydration

 Dehydrated infants require urgent medical attention.

 Lethargic, malnourished, or underfed infants require adequate calories and hydration before they will breastfeed well.

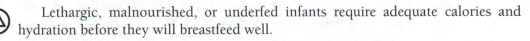 Hyperactivity or irritability related to feeding

Hyperactivity or excessive irritability is abnormal in the healthy, full-term infant but may be seen in the preterm, sick, or neurologically impaired infant who has trouble transitioning smoothly between states and filtering stimuli. Signs of stress among these infants may include:

- Rapid change of state from crying to deep sleep, for example, or from drowsy to hyperalert

- Color changes of the skin: blanching (whitening) or erythema (reddening)

- Vomiting

- Irregular respiration

- Changes in tone

- Apnea

 Hyperactivity or increased irritability is abnormal and requires further evaluation. Suggested physiologic reasons of hyperactivity and/or irritability include:

- Hypoglycemia. Low blood sugar levels may cause infants to act jittery and disorganized at the breast.

- Exposure to drugs. Medications such as labor and medication drugs, prescription or over-the-counter medications, or illegal drugs may pass from mother to infant, resulting in hyperactivity and irritability.

- Reaction to whey in the mother's diet from cow's milk she has consumed.

- Congenital conditions such as a neurologic impairment.

- Prematurity.

- Pain, either current or remembered.

- Illness.

There also may be behavioral reasons for the infant becoming hyperactive and/or irritable before or during breastfeeding. For example:

- The infant may have pain related to the feeding position. Possible sources of pain include birth injuries resulting from forceps and vacuum extraction, cephalohematoma (swelling under the surface of the scalp), torticollis (stiff neck), and broken clavicle. The infant shown in Color Plate 5–3 has cephalohematoma, which may affect its ability to suck correctly.

- The infant may be exhibiting oral aversion from remembered deep suctioning, diagnostic, or therapeutic procedures.

- The infant may be reacting to being forced onto the breast or being held in a forceful, tentative, or uncomfortable way.

 Helping the infant to transition to active alert or quite alert by swaddling or letting the infant cuddle skin-to-skin with the mother may be helpful once the possible reasons for the irritability are discovered and appropriately handled.

Assessment of infant's response to breastfeeding

The infant should feed to satiation, release the breast, and show signs of satisfaction. On occasion, the infant will initiate feeding, but not reach the point of satiation. Possible indicators of feeding problems related to the infant's response are discussed next.

Infant is unable to sustain the feeding

If the infant exhibits feeding cues, is in the appropriate state to feed, and latches on to the breast, but either falls asleep early in the feeding or lies passively at the breast, transfer of an adequate amount of milk is unlikely. When this behavior occurs repeatedly, possible reasons include:

- Malnutrition
- Dehydration
- Jaundice
- Prematurity
- An as-yet undiagnosed condition such as hypoglycemia or neurologic impairment
- A congenital condition such as short or tight lingual frenulum, cleft palate, etc.
- Poor positioning of the infant at the breast such that the nipple is not adequately stretched to facilitate let-down
- Inadequate flow of milk due to low supply of milk
- Infant is not hungry (must be verified by adequate weight gain if this is a chronic problem)

 The mother may incorrectly believe that brief feedings ending repeatedly with a sleeping infant are adequate. Estimation of breast milk intake with a digital scale can assist in determining the quantity of milk transferred.

Infant acts fretful or discontented at the breast

If the infant exhibits feeding cues, is in the appropriate state to feed, latches on to the breast but fusses and frets rather than sucking, releases the breast, or stays passively in the nursing position, transfer of an adequate amount of milk is unlikely. Reasons for this behavior include:

- Chronic underfeeding
- Malnutrition
- Reaction to too much milk or too forceful let-down for the infant (in this case, choking usually accompanies the fretting)
- Infant is not hungry (must be verified by adequate weight gain if this is a chronic problem)
- Pain related with feeding (e.g., the infant with thrush—candida or yeast infection of the mouth)
- Impending or existing illness in the infant
- Immaturity
- Neurologic impairment
- Lack of flow/diminished flow due to low milk supply and/or inhibited oxytocin response
- Poor positioning of the infant at the breast such that the nipple is not adequately stretched to facilitate let-down
- Undiagnosed condition including maternal breast cancer
- Discomfort with the breastfeeding position due to womb position or birth trauma
- Infant preference for artificial nipples

 Early identification and intervention directed at decreasing fretful or discontented behavior may prevent more serious feeding problems.

Infant is unsatisfied after being removed from breast

The unsatisfied infant ends the feeding with clenched fists, furrowed brow, and fussiness and without transferring sufficient milk. Reasons may include:

- Improper latch such that effective feeding did not occur
- Low milk supply or milk flow
- Colic-like reaction to whey in mother's diet
- Premature ending of the feeding

There is a popular idea that infants transfer 90% of the milk in the first 4 or 5 minutes. Although this may be accurate for some infants, it may not be true for any particular infant. Feeding should have the goal of transferring sufficient milk to sustain the infant and should not be limited or directed by the clock.

Infant continues suckling—long feedings with low amounts of milk transfer

Long feedings (more than 30 minutes) may be an early sign of breastfeeding problems or may be characteristic of the mother and infant's breastfeeding style. In order to assess the milk transfer, check before and after weights with a precise digital scale with breast milk intake function. Long feedings with low milk transfer may be due to:

- Insufficient amounts of milk available.

- Insufficient flow due to poor nipple stretching or other let-down inhibition.
- Position of the infant at the breast.
- Immaturity. Preterm and immature infants require long resting times during the feeding. Limiting the duration of the feeding will compromise the amount of milk the infant receives. The feedings should increase in efficiency as the infant matures.
- Congenital anomaly of the infant such as cleft lip, palate, Trisomy 21 (Down Syndrome).

 Breastfeeding sessions with a preterm, immature, or congenitally affected infant usually take considerably longer than sessions with other infants. Continued assessments and evaluations including frequent weight checks and pediatric supervision should always be part of the treatment plan.

- Infant desires more physical contact than provided during feedings.

 If the pattern developed by the mother and infant is such that the infant is held for breastfeedings and rarely otherwise, the infant will learn to continue feeding in order to maximize contact with the mother. Holding the infant in between feedings or use of a sling may change this pattern. Continued assessment of milk transfer and weight gain is imperative.

Infant becomes a progressively more weak and apathetic feeder

The otherwise intact infant who, as the days go by, sleeps longer and deeper in between feedings and nurses listlessly with insufficient transfer is at risk for poor growth, malnutrition, and dehydration. The reasons for this progression may include:

- Inadequate supply of milk.
- Inadequate flow of milk.

 Assess milk transfer by taking before and after weights using a precise scale with breast milk intake function.

- Poor start at breastfeeding. An infant who is underfed for the first days after birth because of restrictive hospital routines may be too lethargic to catch up even when the milk supply becomes copious.
- Malnutrition.
- Dehydration. Infants who are inadequately fed become poor feeders and increase their risk of malnutrition and dehydration.
- Undiagnosed condition.

 Progressive decline in the ability to feed or feeding performance may be the first sign of an as-yet undiagnosed condition. Further prompt medical evaluation by a diagnostician is imperative.

Infant refuses to feed

Evaluation of the infant who is reported to "refuse" to nurse should include a medical assessment of the infant. The infant should also be assessed while being offered the breast in a variety of positions and in a variety of settings. The assessment should include observation of the infant's state and energy level. Assess whether the infant is:

- Unable to feed, or
- Refuses to feed.

Evaluate the possibilities such as lethargy or irritability. The infant who refuses to nurse may do so on one breast or both breasts, but typically a position can be found such that the infant will nurse well sometimes on at least one breast. The infant who consistently refuses to feed may be unable to feed.

 It is important to assure adequate nutrition while assessing the feeding difficulty of an infant who refuses the breast. The initial problem of an infant who refuses the breast can become complicated with malnutrition, dehydration, apathy, and lethargy. An infant may refuse the breast for these reasons:

- The infant has been forcefully put to the breast previously.
- The infant's womb position has limited the nursing positions that feel comfortable.
- The infant's birth injuries (bruising to head or neck, fractured clavicle, and so on) cause the infant to feel pain or discomfort when put to the breast.
- The infant's mother is uncomfortable physically or emotionally with breastfeeding and interprets this discomfort as the infant's refusal to feed.
- The infant's previous experiences with painful diagnostic or therapeutic mouth procedures have left it with oral aversive behavior.
- The infant has other symptoms of a diagnosed or yet to be diagnosed neurological problem.
- The infant has a soft palate cleft or other mouth anomaly.
- The infant is blind or has another physical challenge that has not yet been diagnosed.
- The mother has low breast function.
- The mother has undiagnosed breast cancer—"Goldsmith's sign" (Goldsmith, 1974; Saber et al., 1996).

 An infant that consistently refuses to nurse on one breast has been linked with breast cancer diagnosis in the mother in the 5 years following. The mother should be referred for medical evaluation.

Assessment of infant's interactivity in relation to feeding

During a feeding the infant should be observed to:
- Become increasingly relaxed
- Respond to changes in the flow of milk with a variety of sucking patterns
- Transfer sufficient milk
- End the feeding spontaneously
    The infant who is unable to achieve this level of interactivity may be:
- Hyperactive
- Lethargic

👁 ❓ ⚖ The infant's response during feeding

- How does the infant respond to the sight and smell of the breast?
- How does the infant respond to changes in milk flow?
- Is the infant able to re-attach after loosing the nipple?
- Has the infant transferred sufficient milk?

The observer should also consider:

- Whether the infant is being put to the breast in an inappropriate state
- Whether the infant has been exposed to drugs or medications
- Whether the infant has a diagnosed or undiagnosed congenital condition that affects its ability to interact with the environment

Breastfeeding should be a pleasurable experience for both mother and infant. Normal infant reactions to breastfeeding in the early weeks may include:

- Looking up at the mother
- Wrapping his or her arms around the breast
- Patting or massaging the breast
- Making cooing sounds
- Flailing his or her arms and legs and making rooting motions when close to the mother or anticipating a feeding

 Infants who avert their gaze or never seek faces or objects in the alert states, lie passively at the breast, or have aversive behavior from the beginning of a feeding may have undiagnosed problems unrelated to breastfeeding or may be exhibiting early signs of malnutrition and/or dehydration. Further evaluation and pediatric supervision are imperative.

Performance related to the infant's neuromuscular capacity and ability

Impaired neurologic and/or muscular functioning impacts feeding. Impaired performance may be temporary or permanent. Infants may:

- Have congenital anomalies affecting the neurological or muscular system
- Have had birth trauma such as forceps or vacuum extraction
- Have had exposure to drugs or medications
- Have had a central nervous system insult
- Have had an unusual intra-uterine position
- Have a systemic illness

  Assessment of feeding cues

The infant with permanent or temporary neuromuscular impairment or the underfed infant may not be able to manifest the expected feeding cues. Instead, the infant may consistently demonstrate avoidance behaviors such as:

- Gaze aversion
- Sneezing
- Yawning
- Hiccuping
- Vomiting
- Finger spaying
- Airplaning (arms held stiffly out to the side)
- Stiffening

- Unusual crying (high pitched or inconsolable or weak)

The infant may:

- Become hyperalert in reaction to his or her anticipation of the feeding
- Fall into a deep sleep

The neuromuscularly impaired infant may be unable to coordinate its rooting reflex with approaching the breast, or the rooting reflex may not be observed or observed only occasionally. Crying may be seen as the infant changes from one state to another, and the infant may be hypersensitive to "normal" stimuli such as noise and light.

 Care should be taken to assure that breastfeeding takes place with a minimum of stimulation.

Feeding cues may be absent or so subtle that they are observed only with very close observation. This is often the case with certain congenital conditions such as Trisomy 21 (Down Syndrome).

The neuromuscularly impaired infant may also be disorganized such that placement at the breast evokes feeding cues rather than feeding behaviors. The infant may need extra time skin-to-skin prior to the feeding or familiarizing at the breast prior to nursing.

 Does the infant respond to feeding cues initiated by the mother? The mother may stroke the infant gently and evenly on both sides of the head, progressing toward the lips. Gentle stroking around the lips may evoke lip smacking, mouth seeking, and other pre-feeding behaviors.

 Assessment of infant's desire to feed

Placing the neurologically or muscularly impaired infant at the breast may not initiate feeding behaviors or the behaviors may be delayed. An infant who has had multiple mouth examinations or therapies may be averse to feeding. Desire may be muted by:

- Previous trauma especially involving the face and mouth
- Drug and medication effects
- A congenital condition such as Trisomy 21 (Down Syndrome)
- A delay in feeding, especially if the infant is also compromised in any way (for example, already underfed)
- Infection or impending illness

Lack of desire to feed may also be a sign of disorganization on the part of the infant. The infant's energy may be misplaced (sucking on hands or a pacifier) or the infant may fail to progress from the gape into suckling because of disorientation (inability to locate the nipple). Infants whose mothers have had epidural medications in labor are more likely to be disorganized when attempting to breastfeed (Sepkoski et al., 1992).

Assessment of infant's orientation to the breast

An infant who is unable to orient to the breast to feed needs to be assessed as:

- Having appropriate motions, but is unable to achieve the goal of feeding. This may be related to maternal labor medications (Righard et al., 1990; Sepkoski et al., 1992).

or

- Lacking appropriate motions to achieve the goal of feeding. This may be due to:
  ○ Immaturity, prematurity
  ○ Drugs or medications affecting the infant
  ○ A congenital condition, diagnosed or undiagnosed

  If the cause of the infant's lack of appropriate motions is known, interventions should be undertaken to compensate and achieve the most optimum feeding possible. If the infant is observed to lack appropriate motions and the infant's condition is undiagnosed, further medical evaluation is imperative.

Assessment of the infant's coordination in relation to breastfeeding

Inability to coordinate the suck-swallow-breathe activity of breastfeeding is associated with prematurity as well as neuromuscular impairment. The premature infant may not be permitted to attempt at-breast feedings until the suck-swallow-breathe is observed, although research indicates that prematurely born infants are capable of nutritive sucking and increasing their milk consumption at a low postmenstrual age (Nyqvist, 2001). The uncoordinated infant may:

- Choke or gag at the breast
- Pull away to breathe
- Suck but not swallow
- Suck only when triggered by a swallow

  These behaviors may be related to:
- Immaturity or prematurity
- Medication effects
- A congenital condition diagnosed or as yet undiagnosed

Assessment of the infant's muscle tone in relation to breastfeeding

Hypotonia, or low muscle tone, is the most consistent abnormality to be observed in the neonatal neurologic exam (Tappero & Honeyfield, 1996), so it is not surprising to find hypotonia among the population of breastfeeding infants (Color Plate 5–4). However, any generalized increase or decrease in tone is significant as it may indicate a central nervous system insult or a systemic illness.

 It is imperative that the infant receives prompt medical evaluation if any increase or decrease in muscle tone is observed.

The hypotonic infant may:

- Be premature or immature
- Be malnourished
- Be dehydrated
- Be affected by drugs or medications
- Have a diagnosed or undiagnosed congenital condition such a Trisomy 21 (Down Syndrome), cardiac anomaly, etc.

- Have had a central nervous system insult
- Have a systemic illness such as infantile botulism, sepsis, etc.

 The hypotonic infant is floppy, flaccid, and low-toned with a weak suck. The infant may have poor head control and be unable to latch onto the breast and maintain the latch without assistance. Swaddling the infant in a flexed position may be helpful. The infant may exhibit subtle or no feeding cues, requiring the mother to initiate the feeding with gentle stroking of the face and lips.

Hypertonicity, or high muscle tone, is a less common finding than hypotonia in the newborn period (Tappero & Honeyfield, 1996) (Color Plate 5–5). The infant with hypertonia may be seen as arching its back, maintaining a stiff posture. The hypertonic infant often:

- Is easily over-stimulated
- Leans away from the mother rather than moving toward her warmth
- Is difficult to comfort

Hypertonicity may be associated with:

- Previous negative or painful experiences at the breast
- Neurologic damage
- Bacterial meningitis
- Severe hypoxic-ischemic brain damage
- Massive intraventricular hemorrage
- Tetanus

 The hypertonic infant responds to breastfeeding as too much stimulation. In addition to arching, it may become increasingly stressed at the contact. Mothers have successfully nursed hypertonic infants in low light, with very little noise, and with the only touching between the mother and infant being the infant's mouth to the mother's breast.

 Infants who are noted to exhibit sustained or chronic high muscle tone should be referred for medical evaluation.

Assessment of infant output

Infant urination and stooling patterns are indicators of the adequacy of milk transfer. After the first few days of life, it is expected that the young newborn will have a minimum of three stools and six urinations daily.

 Infants producing less than three stools and/or six urinations daily should be evaluated immediately for adequacy of milk transfer.

Unusual urine

The breastfed infant's urine should not be concentrated. It should be light in color and copious in amount after the first few days. There should be no smell.

Brick-dust urine:

- Appears in newborns as brick colored
- Is associated with insufficient milk transfer and dehydration
- Is indicative of uric acid crystals (Color Plate 5–6)
- Is sometimes mistaken for blood

Brick dust urine is an ominous sign. Infants are often hospitalized for rehydration while the mother's milk supply is evaluated.

Concentrated urine:

- Is dark in color
- Has an ammonia odor
- Is indicative of dehydration

 Concentrated urine is a sign of inadequate feeding, A medical evaluation of the infant, a breastfeeding evaluation, and an evaluation of the adequacy of the mother's milk supply are imperative.

Unusual stools

Blood in the stools can occur for several reasons:

- The infant may have anal fissures.
- The infant may be allergic/have a reaction to a protein the infant or mother has eaten.
- The infant may be bleeding internally.

 The breastfed infant rarely has diarrhea (however, normal breastfed infant stools are sometimes mistaken for diarrhea). A medical evaluation is imperative if diarrhea is suspected in a nursing infant.

Foul-smelling stools

 The breastfed infant's stools are sweet-smelling. Foul-smelling stools are indicative of the need for a medical evaluation.

Yellow greenish mucous stools:

- Are related to insufficient stretching of the nipple during nursing, and so there is less oxytocin
- May be of concern if they do not disappear with improved breastfeeding technique

 Mucous stools should resolve in 24–48 hours with improved breastfeeding positioning or nipple stretching prior to nursing. If they continue, medical evaluation is imperative.

Frothy stools may be associated with diagnosed or as-yet undiagnosed congenital conditions.

 Medical evaluation of the infant is imperative if the stools are frothy.

SECTION III

Assessing the Mother

CHAPTER 6

Optimal Breastfeeding—The Mother's Role

CHAPTER 7

Possible Anomolies Related to the Breastfeeding Mother

Optimal Breastfeeding— The Mother's Role

6

Mammals have mammary glands

Human beings are mammals and, by definition, female mammals make milk for their infants. Knowing about the making of milk in the mammary glands and the delivery of milk in other species is fascinating, but of limited helpfulness in understanding human milk production or delivery. Kangaroos, for example, have two mammary glands, or "teats," (just like humans) but make two very different milks simultaneously, one for the very immature, newly born infant in the pouch and another for the "toddler" who hops over to nurse. Domesticated mammals—dogs and cats—have rows of mammary glands. There is a vast difference between the physiologic production of milk for one or two offspring and the commercial production of animal milk, such as cow's milk. Therefore, management of lactation in dairy mammals is not directly applicable to a human mother and her infant.

All humans have mammary glands. Nipples are evident in infants at birth, as seen in Figure 6–1. In males, the mammary glands stop developing, while girls continue to develop during puberty under the influence of the hormones estrogen and progesterone.

During adolescence, the female breast develops from the nipple into the breast, forming first the main ducts, then the smaller ducts that end with the milk-producing cells called alveoli, as seen in Figure 6–2. With each menstrual cycle, shifts in hormonal balances result in further mammary development (Figure 6–3). The hormones present during pregnancy (specifically placental lactogen, prolactin, and chorionic gonadotropin) cause accelerated growth and maturity of the mammary glands. Figure 6–4 shows an example. The breast is thought to contain between 15 and 25 of these duct networks, which are referred to as lobes. Each main duct has an opening in the nipple called the nipple pore.

For reference purposes, the breast is divided into four quadrants, as illustrated in Figure 6–5:

- Upper outer quadrant
- Lower outer quadrant
- Lower inner quadrant
- Upper inner quadrant

FIGURE 6–1   Child's
breast.

*Used with permission. © Health
Education Associates*

Child

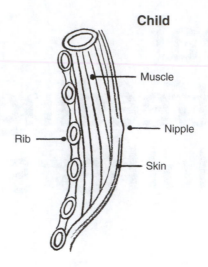

FIGURE 6–2   Developing
adolescent breast.

*Used with permission. © Health
Education Associates*

Adolescent

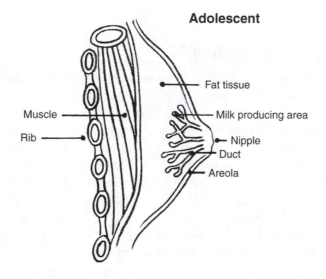

FIGURE 6–3   Adult breast.

*Used with permission. © Health
Education Associates*

Adult

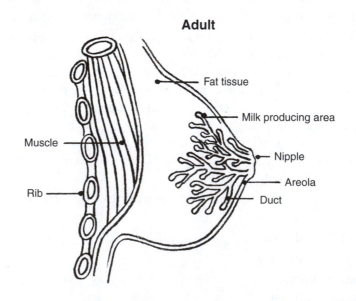

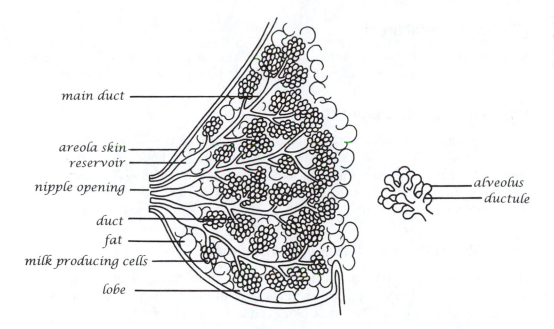

FIGURE 6–4 Cross-section of lactating breast.
Used with permission. ©Healthy Children 2000 Project

main duct

areola skin
reservoir

nipple opening

duct

fat

milk producing cells

lobe

alveolus

ductule

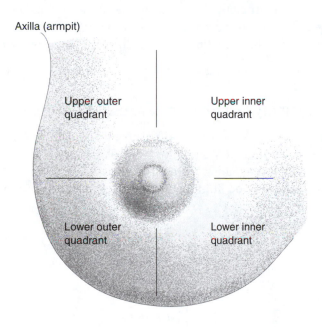

Axilla (armpit)

Upper outer
quadrant

Upper inner
quadrant

Lower outer
quadrant

Lower inner
quadrant

FIGURE 6–5 Quadrants of the breast.
Used with permission. © Health Education Associates

Functioning breasts and nipples

  Breast size

Fat surrounds the duct networks in the breast and gives the breast its shape and size. The size characteristics of the mature woman's breast vary from one woman to another, but the size of the breast is not related to the ability to produce sufficient milk for the infant.

Symmetrical breasts

A woman's breasts are never identical, but optimally should be comparable in shape and size. The size and shape of each breast should be very similar to the other.

Compressible breast tissue

The breast must optimally be soft enough to conform to the shape of the infant's mouth during suckling. The infant's lips are to be positioned over the collecting sinuses, which are portions of the ducts that enlarge during suckling. The location of these collecting sinuses may or may not correlate with the areola (the darker portion of the breast surrounding the nipple).

Visible veins with an overall breast pattern

Preparation for lactation under the influence of the hormones of pregnancy includes an increase in the blood supply to the breasts resulting in observable (blue) veins that are patterned on both breasts. Color Plate 6–1 shows an example.

Intact, smooth epithelium on the breast

The breast surface, or epithelial layer, is normally unbroken, as seen in Figure 6–6. Aside from nipples and Montgomery glands, optimally there should be no lumps or raised areas, nor should there be dimples. Stretch marks may be visible and normal.

 Identify any scar or other marking on the breast and determine its cause.

Montgomery glands, or tubercles, on the areola

Montgomery's glands, or tubercles, are located around the nipple on the areola. Color Plate 6–2 shows very prominent Montgomery glands. These glands become larger and more noticeable during pregnancy. Women may describe them as "goose bumps." These glands produce a unique fluid that is both antimicrobial and lubricating.

FIGURE 6–6 External anatomy of the breast.

Used with permission. ©Healthy Children 2000 Project

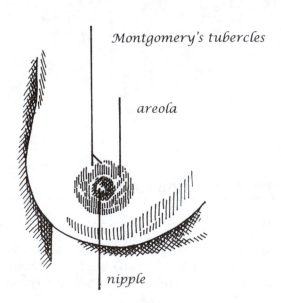

Montgomery's tubercles

areola

nipple

Evidences of secretion from the Montgomery glands are:

- A sheen on the areola
- The mother's report of water beading up on the skin of the areola and breast during bathing

Montgomery gland secretion may be first noticed in late pregnancy, although the enlargement of the glands may be observed earlier in pregnancy.

Evenly pigmented, wrinkled nipple surface

Optimally, the nipple surface is evenly pigmented with no signs of redness, abrasion, fissures, cracks, blisters, blebs, pus, blood, or mucus. The nipple skin surface is wrinkled, having the potential to expand two to three times its resting length. There may be as many as 25 nipple pores burrowed in the tip of the nipple, although most mothers report 7–9 sprays during a feeding, indicating that not all of the milk systems are in use during lactation.

Presence of milk

Milk may be seen flowing from the mother's breast, collected in containers, and spit or vomited up by the infant. Milk may have a different appearance according to the stage of lactation but may also be colored by the mother's diet and drugs. Color Plate 6–3 compares the appearance of colostrum, mature breastmilk, and artificial infant milk (formula). The mother's milk should be appropriate for her state of lactation:

- Colostrum. Colostrum is produced under the influence of the hormones of lactation, appears mid-pregnancy, and continues to be secreted for 7–10 days after the infant is born, although it is mixed with copious amounts of mature milk beginning on the second or third day. Colostrum is yellowish or yellow orange and thick.
- Transitional milk. Transitional milk is the milk that contains both colostrum and mature milk. This milk created by lactogenesis II, begins to appear around the second or third day postpartum. Copious in amount, it has the yellow, yellow orange, thick quality of colostrum and the whitish blue constituents of mature milk.
- Mature milk. Mature milk contains no colostrum. Mature milk appears thin and watery and is often whitish blue in color. Breastmilk may also normally appear yellowish or greenish, due to vitamins or supplements in the mother's diet.

Patent milk ducts in the breast and nipple

Each milk duct network should terminate at the end of the nipple, allowing for the passage of milk from the milk-making cells, the alveoli, to the infant. Evidence of patent (open) milk ducts includes:

- Colostrum leakage during the last trimester of pregnancy (although a mother may have patent ducts and not leak colostrum)
- Ability to express droplets of milk with gentle hand massage (see Color Plate 6–4)
- Milk leaking between feedings during lactation
- Milk spraying or leaking from the opposite breast during nursing
- Milk transfer measured by an increase in infant weight taken before and after nursing

Evidence of innervation of the breast and nipple

The breasts are innervated by the fourth, fifth, and sixth intercostal nerves; the highly sensitive nipple and areola are primarily innervated by the fourth intercostal nerve. Stimulation of the nipple sends a message via the nerves to the pituitary to make and secrete hormones that work to produce and deliver milk. The stimulus of the warm, wet mouth of the infant results in optimal levels of prolactin, which stimulates the production of milk in the breast. Oxytocin, secreted in response to stimuli including nipple stretching and the infant's hands kneading the breast, triggers the delivery of the milk through a process called "let-down" or "milk ejection." The nipple should optimally be responsive to touch, everting in response to stroking, finger manipulation, cold, and/or sexual stimulation.

  ## Removal of milk to maintain cellular integrity of milk-making cells

In response to frequent and rapid removal of milk, the alveolar cells produce more milk. Increased pressure on the milk-making cells changes the cell configuration so that less milk is made. Cellular integrity is partially dependent on lack of pressure on the milk, making cells:

- Internally from sufficient and efficient milk removal
- Externally from nonrestrictive clothing such as the bra
- Both because increased milk retention in the breast enlarges the breast and a formerly adequate bra may become restrictive

  ## Everted, tubular-shaped nipples

The everted nipple is stimulated during suckling and triggers an increase in the secretion of the hormone prolactin, which stimulates the milk-making cells to produce milk. The nipple is stretched far back into the infant's mouth and formed into a tubular shape. Nipple stretching causes the secretion of the hormone oxytocin, which in turn contracts the smooth muscle (myoepithelial) cells surrounding the milk-making (alveolar) cells.

  ## Intact neuromuscular ability to position infant

The mother and infant work together to find the optimal position for breastfeeding, and the mother should be comfortable either sitting or lying down without straining. The position selected should allow for efficient milk transfer without nipple pain. The mother should be able to maintain the position for the feeding.

If the position of the infant is incorrect or painful, the mother should break the seal either by inserting her clean finger in the corner of the infant's mouth or pressing gently against her breast.

If the infant loses the nipple during a feeding, the mother and infant may need to work to re-latch.

Maternal hormones optimally support lactation

In the postpartum, lactation is achieved by a specific and unique combination of hormonal events:

- Pregnancy has prepared the breast for lactation through the influence of the primary hormones prolactin, estrogen, and progesterone. Colostrum is produced beginning in pregnancy; this is called "lactogenesis I."

- A rapid decline in progesterone and estrogen occurs with the complete delivery of the placenta. During pregnancy, progesterone binds to receptor sites in the breast, blocking prolactin from triggering the manufacture of mature milk. When progesterone levels fall after the placenta is delivered, rising prolactin levels in response to nipple stimulation trigger the production of mature milk. This is called "lactogenesis II." Copious milk is secreted by the third day postpartum as a result of this hormonal change, "lactogenesis II." The milk is a combination of colostrum and mature milk—"transitional milk" for 7–10 days. Lactogenesis III is the ongoing production of milk supported by continued prolactin secretion with nipple stimulation and lack of pressure on the milk-making cells.

- A functioning oxytocin secretion occurs in response to nipple stretching and/or a stimulus response reaction triggered by the mother smelling, touching, hearing, remembering, or thinking about the infant. Evidence of oxytocin release may include:
  - The mother's report of a "tingling" sensation in the breasts
  - Milk leaking from the opposite breast when the infant is feeding
  - The mother's report of uterine cramping as the infant feeds
  - The infant's increased frequency of swallowing
  - Leakage of milk between feeds
  - The mother's feeling of well-being after a feeding

Some mothers are unaware of any of these signs. Other mothers may misconstrue lack of strong sensations as a sign of inadequate milk.

Figure 6–7 summarizes the pathway and roles of prolactin and oxytocin.

Other physiologic indicators

Normal levels of iron

Normal iron levels allow women to feel well and have well-oxygenated cells. Women with iron-deficiency anemia are at greater risk of recurrent mastitis and physiologic fatigue.

Normal levels of thyroid hormone

Normal thyroid levels are essential for adequate milk production. Both low and high thyroid levels have been associated with milk supply problems.

FIGURE 6–7 Prolactin and oxytocin.

Used with permission. ©Healthy Children 2000 Project

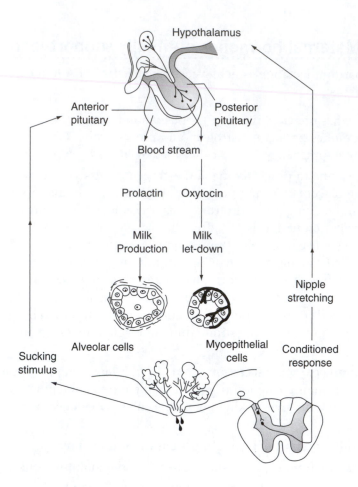

(?) Normal uterine discharge

Uterine discharge after birth is an indicator of the healing of the uterus after birth. Pernoll (1991) states the predictable sequence expected:

- Lochia rubia is the blood-tinged uterine discharge post-delivery that includes shreds of tissue and decidua.

- Lochia serosa is the paler, clearer uterine discharge that is seen after a few days.

- Lochia alba normally appears in the second and third postpartum week. The discharge is thicker, muchoid, and yellowish, containing predominantly leukocytes and degenerated dedicual cells.

- Lochial secretions cease as healing nears completion, usually by the fifth week.

Educational expectation of the mother

It is important for the mother (and her support people) to understand the basic concepts of lactation:

- Formula feeding is less desirable both on public health and individual levels.

- Infants should be fed on cue, not by the clock, 8 to 12 times a day, at first.

- How to make milk on an ongoing basis. The infant is expected to gain weight at a rate of ½–1 ounce per day and have frequent bowel movements and urination.

- Problems, including sleepy infants or poor feeders, as well as breast problems, should be investigated.
- Help is available if breastfeeding seems difficult, hurts, or if there are any problems. Mothers should be made aware of, and encouraged to seek out, community resources.

👁 ❓ Behavioral expectations of the mother

It is expected that the mother will put her understanding of lactation into action. She is:

- Able to offer the breast to the infant as needed. If this is not possible, the mother is able to remove milk by hand expression or pumping for later feeding.
- Willing to remove milk frequently and sufficiently.

👁 ❓ Optimal maternal response to breastfeeding

The mother reports that she:
- Feels only tugging at her breast during the feeding (no pain)
- Is confident in her continuing ability to make milk
- Feels supported in her decision to breastfeed
- Has a feeling of well-being
- Enjoys breastfeeding, as seen in Figure 6–8

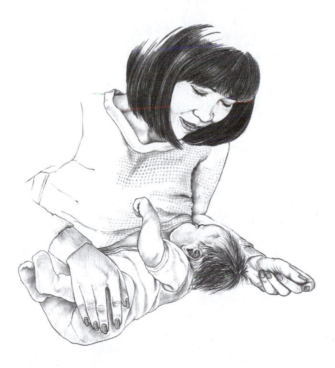

FIGURE 6–8 Breastfeeding is an enjoyable experience for mother and baby.

Used with permission. © Health Education Associates

Possible Anomalies Related to the Breastfeeding Mother

Assessment of the breasts

   Size of breast

Size of the breast is proportionately unimportant relative to breast function. The milk storage capacity of the breast cannot be judged by the increase in breast size during pregnancy (Cregan & Hartmann, 1999). Essential considerations to be evaluated in an assessment are:

- Confirmation of functional milk-making tissue
- Patent ducts
- Appropriate innervation
- Frequent and efficient removal of milk

Gigantomastia (extreme breast overgrowth) of pregnancy has been reported, with breasts increasing in size up to 25 pounds each (VanHeerden et al., 1988). The cause of this massive growth of the breasts during pregnancy is unknown and there are no reports of lactation with this condition.

 Absence of breast changes during pregnancy

Mothers who report no changes in their breasts during pregnancy may signal a concern regarding their ability to produce milk. However, some women do not experience these normal breast changes until the immediate postpartum period. If a mother reports no evidence of breast changes during either pregnancy or the immediate postpartum period, breastfeeding should be monitored closely so that the infant does not become nutritionally compromised.

Absence of breast enlargement, breast tenderness, increased skin pigmentation of the areola, increased veining of the breasts, and/or enlargement of the Montgomery glands during pregnancy and immediate postpartum period may be of concern as indication of inadequate glandular tissue.

(?) (👁) Absence of breast changes postpartum

Absence of leaking of milk and feelings of fullness as the mother's milk "comes in" may be of concern regarding insufficient glandular tissue.

(⚠)   Pediatric supervision of this mother's infant, including frequent weight checks, is vital.

(👁) (?) (📁) One breast

It is possible to fully breastfeed an infant with only one optimally functioning breast. Only one functioning breast may be present congenitally (amastia), following injury or trauma, or following mastectomy or other significant unilateral breast surgery.

When a mother has had a partial or radical mastectomy on one breast, breastfeeding may be possible on the remaining, intact breast. Women who have had reconstructive surgery have had functional breast tissue replaced with other prosthetic material. If the mother has had therapeutic doses of radiation, milk-making capacity may be severely diminished. It is important to ask if either breast has been exposed to therapeutic doses of radiation.

(⚠)   During lactogenesis stage II, abundant milk may be produced in both breasts because of the hormonal changes of pregnancy and the delivery of the placenta. This does not mean that sufficient milk during ongoing milk production (lactogenesis III) will necessarily follow.

(💼)   The mother may need to be taught comfort strategies if milk cannot flow out of the affected breast and the pressure becomes painful. Removing a small amount of milk by submerging the breasts in water, or by gentle hand expression, may be helpful.

(⚠)   The infant of a mother with a non-functional breast will require frequent weight checks and close pediatric supervision as the other breast may not function optimally.

(👁) (?) (📁) More than two breasts or nipples—polymastia: Accessory breasts or super-numerary breasts or nipples

Additional breast tissue and nipples may occur on the body along the "milk line" that extends from the axilla (armpit) to the groin. Figure 7–1 indicates the locations where accessory breast and/or nipple tissue has been identified. Small areas of accessory breast tissue may fill up with milk on the second or third day postpartum but, because these super-numerary breasts are rarely fully functional, there are usually no or few ducts that would enable the milk to exit. Milk pressure builds and eventually the tissue involutes or "dries up." Occasionally, what the mother thought was a mole is actually a supernumerary, or extra, nipple that increases in size during pregnancy and may or may not produce milk. The mother shown in Color Plate 7–1 has a supernumerary nipple on her left areola that did not interfere with latch-on, suck, or breastfeeding.

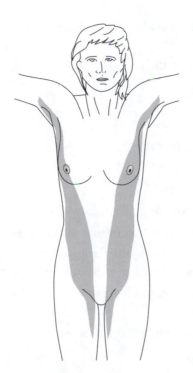

FIGURE 7–1 Shaded area indicates possible locations of accessory breast and/or nipple tissue.

  ### Asymmetrical breasts associated with inadequate glandular tissue

Breasts are usually slightly asymmetrical (different in size and shape), but markedly asymmetrical breasts are always cause for close follow-up. Infants of such mothers should have frequent weight checks (Huggins, 2000; Neifert, 1985). Asymmetrical breasts, such as those shown in Color Plate 7–2, may indicate that there is also insufficient glandular tissue, although there are reports of mothers who have markedly asymmetrical breasts that produce adequate milk.

Of increased concern are mothers with asymmetrical breasts that appear tubular in shape and/or the mother's report of no breast changes during pregnancy or in the immediate postpartum period. Asymmetrical breasts may be congenital or a result of trauma, radiation therapy, insertion of a chest tube in infancy, or preadolescent breast surgery such as biopsy.

   ### Underdeveloped breasts (micromastia)

Abnormally small, immature-looking breasts may indicate lack of glandular tissue or hormonal imbalance.

 Infants whose mother's breasts are observed to be markedly underdeveloped require frequent weight checks and close pediatric follow-up.

  ### Scars and marks on the breast

The presence of any visible marks on the breast indicates the need to determine their cause. Causes of such marks may include:

- Indentation marks from:
  - Tight bra or other restrictive clothing, as shown in Color Plate 7–3

- ° Breast shells, nipple shields, pump flanges, or other equipment (see Color Plate 7–4)

 External compression of the breast is related to an increased chance of breast - problems.

- • Scars from:
  - ° Breast reduction surgery
  - ° Breast augmentation surgery
  - ° Breast biopsy and surgery
  - ° Past trauma to the breast
- • Bruising or abrasion from ongoing trauma from:
  - ° Incorrect breastfeeding positioning and attachment, as shown in Color Plate 7–5
  - ° Misuse of pump (e.g., pulling the flange off of the breast before turning off the pump, using a non-automatic pump without appropriate suction breaks, etc.)
  - ° Other trauma to chest (e.g., blows to the chest from sports injury or car accident, etc.)
- • Signs of inflammation, infection, or abscess

Rigid or noncompressible areola and breast—Generalized hardness

In order for the infant to effectively draw the nipple and breast tissue into his or her mouth, the area of the breast behind the nipple should be soft and pliable enough to compress into the infant's mouth. A rigid or noncompressible breast or areola may be related to:

- • Unilateral or bilateral engorgement due to inadequate removal of milk. This may be observed from the second to the tenth day postpartum, and is usually preventable by adequate, frequent feedings in the early days. Breast engorgement is characterized by generalized hardness of the breast, even extending into the Tail of Spence (breast tissue extending into the axilla or armpit area). The skin may be warm or hot to the touch and distended to the point of shininess. The mother may have a temperature above normal and feel uncomfortable.
- • Unilateral or bilateral engorgement due to missed feedings. This may be observed any time after the second day postpartum and may be aggravated by inadequate milk removal. It may also be observed at other times when feedings are missed.

 Gentle handling of the breasts is important. Soaking the breasts in a basin of warm water and massaging gently may be a helpful early strategy. Breast pumping with high suction should be avoided until the milk is flowing. The best relief after the hard area has softened is a well-positioned nursing infant.

- • Bilateral fullness of the breast. This may occur in early lactation (days 2–4) and later in lactation if feedings are missed (such as when the infant first sleeps through the night).

 Care should be taken to relieve any breast fullness—pressure on the milk-making cells can reduce the quantity of milk.

- • Bilateral or unilateral fullness of the breast due to inadequate drainage of the lymphatic system (rare).

FIGURE 7–2 Removing a small amount of milk by submerging breasts in water. *Used with permission. ©Health Education Associates*

Removing a small amount of milk via submersion of breasts in water, as seen in Figure 7–2, by hand expression or by pumping may make the areola softer and the breast and nipple more available for the infant. Inadequate drainage of lymph may be secondary to lymphatic system blockage in the axilla. If milk removal does not soften the breast and areolar area, a medical assessment is recommended.

- Unilateral or bilateral fullness or engorgement secondary to breast implants, biopsy, or other trauma restricting the flow of milk. Color Plate 7–6 shows breasts with implants: The right breast is functioning normally in spite of implant. The left breast is painfully engorged secondary to implant, impeding/blocking milk flow. Inspection of the breast for visible signs of breast surgery should always be part of the assessment; however, the mother should also be questioned about surgery involving the breast because an augmentation scar may be hidden in her armpit, navel, or under the heaviness of her breast. The most candid answers will be given if the questions related to elective breast surgery are asked in private. Family members and partners may be unaware of the surgery.

The breasts may have been augmented using a variety of procedures with a range of effects on breastfeeding and human lactation:

- The incision may have been made under the breast and the implant placed under the breast tissue. The scar is visible when the breast is lifted.

- The incision may have been made anywhere on the breast. Scarring from incision can be seen in Color Plate 7–6.

- The incision may have been made around the areola-nipple area (peri-areolar incision). The scar is usually visible at the margin of the pigment change along the edge of the areola. Of concern with this surgical technique is that the ducts leading to the nipple and nerves innervating the nipple may have been severed. This procedure has been shown to have the greatest negative effect on breastfeeding. This incision may also be indicative of breast reduction surgery.

- The incision may have been made across the areola-nipple area. This procedure is disruptive to lactation because the ducts, nerves, and blood supply are negatively altered.

- The incision may have been made in the axilla. The scar may not be visible except on very close inspection. This procedure is less likely to have impact on the ducts, nerves, and blood supply.

- The incision can be made in the umbilicus and the implant threaded up to the breast. The scar may be visible only with very close inspection.

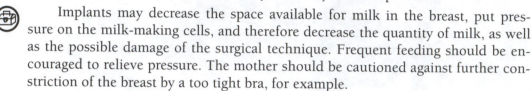 Implants may decrease the space available for milk in the breast, put pressure on the milk-making cells, and therefore decrease the quantity of milk, as well as the possible damage of the surgical technique. Frequent feeding should be encouraged to relieve pressure. The mother should be cautioned against further constriction of the breast by a too tight bra, for example.

Infants of mothers with breast implants should have frequent weight checks with a precise digital scale and close pediatric follow-up.

- Inelastic skin. Surgical scars, trauma, and burns may contribute to lack of skin elasticity. This may make it difficult for the infant to latch on to the breast.

Mothers with inelastic skin should feed their infants regularly to avoid breast fullness, which would further stretch the skin. Comfort measures such as soaking the breasts and hand expression or pumping may be helpful.

If the skin is not pliable enough, pressure on the milk-making cells may diminish the milk supply.

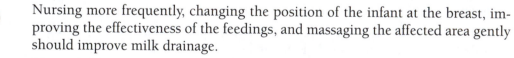 **Raised or hard areas of the breast—lumps**

Any mass detected in the breast during lactation requires prompt evaluation. If the mass does not respond in one of two days to treatments such as increased nursing and removal of possible causes of blockage, further investigation by an appropriate physician is mandatory. With the sophisticated diagnostic techniques available, suppression of lactation is not necessary during diagnostic work-up.

Reasons for hardened or lumpy areas in the breast may include:

- Normal condition of lactating breasts. Lactating breasts are lumpy, but the position of a normal lump generally shifts from nursing to nursing and from day to day.

Nursing more frequently, changing the position of the infant at the breast, improving the effectiveness of the feedings, and massaging the affected area gently should improve milk drainage.

- Plugged duct or clog. A plugged duct or clog is a localized breast problem that presents as a hardened area of the breast, without redness or other flu-like systemic symptoms such as fever or malaise. The area may be tender to the touch. Once the area is drained of milk, normal function returns. Plugged ducts or clogs may be related to:

  ○ Full milk-making cells and ducts that don't drain sufficiently because of poor positioning or inadequate suckling

  ○ Blockage of ducts by cells that have been shed

  ○ Inadequate milk removal because of hurried or infrequent feedings

  ◦ Poor-fitting bra (Color Plate 7–7), pressure from an underwire or other pressure on the area of the breast such as a bunched nightgown

A clog or plugged duct should respond to improved suckling and milk removal. Many mothers report that light breast massage and pointing the infant's chin toward the clog during feeding improves the flow of milk.

A physician should examine any clog that does not respond to interventions in 24–48 hours.

- Abscess or localized collection of pus that is the result of a disintegration of tissue. The abscessed area in the left breast is clearly visible in Color Plate 7–8. An abscess is palpated as a hardened area of the breast that does not move or disappear with increased or improved nursing. The hardened area may be noticed in conjunction with mastitis and there may be a reddened area of skin over the location of the hardened area.

An abscess must drain; it will not resolve in any other way. Drainage may occur by surgery, or by rupture into the duct system, causing the pus to mix with milk or by rupture to the outside. Small abscesses may be drained by fine needle aspiration or larger ones by lancing.

Weaning is rarely indicated in the case of abscess. However, it may be necessary to discontinue breastfeeding temporarily on the affected breast because the location of the abscess is too close to the nipple and areola. During this time, lactation may be maintained by hand expression or by pumping the affected breast. Breastfeeding can continue on the unaffected breast. Systemic antibiotic therapy is also part of the treatment plan.

- Galactocele or milk retention cyst. This hardened area of the breast may be due to milk that has been produced, but for some unknown reason, does not flow from the breast. At first the cyst will be milk-filled. Eventually, because of fluid absorption, the galactocele will contain a more cheesy substance. Ultrasound will show that the galactocele has a similar appearance to milk. Galactoceles may be drained for diagnosis and for mother's comfort; however, breastfeeding with a galactocele is not contraindicated.

- Fibrocystic disease is also called fibrocystic changes of the breast. These palpable lumps in the breast are common in women during their childbearing years. Thought to be due to reactions in the mammary tissue to hormonal shifts during the menstrual cycle, the lumps generally lessen with pregnancy. Symptoms include pain, tenderness, and nodules of varying sizes. Diagnostic procedures include palpation of a lump that moves freely, mammography, and needle aspiration biopsy. Fibrocystic changes are not contraindications for breastfeeding.

- Breast cancer. Two to three percent of women who are diagnosed with breast cancer are either pregnant or lactating (Hoover, 1990). It is recommended that a physician undertake a thorough investigation of a breast mass if:

  ◦ The area shows no decrease in size after 72 hours of treatment

  ◦ There are mastitis-like symptoms (without fever) that are not resolved after a course of antibiotic therapy

  ◦ There is recurrent mastitis-like hardness reappearing at the same location in the breast (Petok, 1995)

  ◦ The shape of the breast or nipple is distorted. Color Plate 7–9 shows the right nipple pulling off center secondary to breast cancer.

- Additional reasons for lumps. There may be other reasons for lumps in the breast that are unrelated to lactation, such as:
  - Breast cysts, which are firm, smooth, freely movable masses
  - Fat necrosis caused by the local destruction of fat cells
  - Lipomas, which are soft, well delineated, and freely movable
  - Hematomas, which occur as a result of trauma

     Each of these conditions has a unique appearance during radiographic diagnostic procedures and usually does not impact breastfeeding.
- Hardened areas of the breast radiating from the areola. When milk is made but cannot exit the breast via the nipple pore, the retained milk may take the shape of the ducts and ductules and creates an enlarged area of the breast. This may be a result of:
  - A surgical procedure that has cut through ducts in the nipple area during a biopsy, lumpectomy, or lancing of an abscess
  - A congenital condition such as a galactocele or ectopic ducts that causes the milk-making cells and ducts to be separated from the nipple pores
  - Surgery that separates the nipple from the breast in breast reduction, or impacts innervation of the nipple as in augmentation procedure, as shown in Color Plate 7–10
  - A burn around the nipple area that has left scar tissue, blocking the nipple pore
  - Other trauma
  - A bleb, or white dot, usually solitary, on the end of the nipple that keeps the duct from draining. Blebs are very difficult to remove. The mother may be in considerable pain, which she describes as "pinpoint pain."

     Blebs often keep reforming even after successful removal. Rarely, the bleb will disappear with active suckling or pumping. Mothers have used warm water soaks and gentle compression to push out the bleb from behind, or a health professional may use a sterile needle to open the bleb.

No visible veins or atypical pattern of veins on the breast

Lack of visible veins or an atypical pattern of veins on the breast at the end of pregnancy and early lactation may indicate a lack of hormonal response in the breast, as would be expected as a normal change of pregnancy. Insufficient development of milk-making tissue may be suspected, especially if the breasts are also asymmetrical.

 If the breast has not responded to the hormones of pregnancy by increasing the blood supply, there is concern that the hormonal pathway may be compromised. Milk production may be diminished.

An atypical pattern of veins on the breast:

- May be normal
- May indicate tumor growth or other pathology
- May be related to inadequate development of glandular tissue
- May be related to past trauma to the breast, including surgery such as breast reduction surgery

An atypical vein pattern should be assessed medically. Breastfeeding infants of mothers with atypical vein patterns should have frequent weight checks and close pediatric supervision.

Enlarged Montgomery glands

Enlarged Montgomery glands may be:

- A normal response to pregnancy and lactation (see Figure 6–2)
- Infected

 Antibiotic therapy may be indicated.

- Injured by the trauma of poor latch, or the rubbing or pressure of gadgets such as breast shells, nipple shields or pump flanges

 Removal of the irritant is necessary.

A herpes lesion on the breast or areola may be described by the mother vaguely as a "sore" and may be mistaken for an infected Montgomery gland. Herpes lesions are painful and blister-like. Culturing the lesion assists differential diagnosis.

Blisters on the breast or areola

Blisters may be related to a variety of factors, such as:

- Herpes simplex virus (Color Plate 7–11)

 Herpes on the breast and areola is a contraindication to breastfeeding. Herpes may be transmitted from the mother's breast to the neonate during breastfeeding with deadly results. Culturing the lesion is necessary to diagnose HSV. If there is any question about whether the sore is an infected Montgomery gland or a HSV lesion in the early weeks postpartum, differential diagnosis is imperative, as herpes can be life threatening to infants.

 Herpes lesions on other parts of the body do not contraindicate breastfeeding; however, they should be covered and every precaution should be taken to avoid the spread of HSV to the vulnerable infant.

- Poor positioning of the infant at the breast

Irritation to the poorly positioned nipple can cause blisters filled with clear fluid. Improving the position of the infant at the breast will minimize the trauma to the nipple skin. The infant may develop a blister on his or her lip for the same reason.

- Poison ivy or other skin condition for which the mother should seek medical therapy.

Poison ivy can occur anywhere on the body that has been in contact with the poison ivy toxin, including the breast. Although there is no danger to the infant from nursing if the mother has poison ivy on her breasts and areola, there is concern that the infant could contribute to a secondary infection on the mother's breast or areola through contact with the already damaged skin. The contents of the poison ivy blisters do not spread the disease.

Breast redness—inflammation

A reddened area of the breast is often indicative of breast inflammation or mastitis. Mastitis can be infective or noninfective.

 Because the symptoms of infective and noninfective mastitis are similar, antibiotics are often prescribed for both types.

Unilateral infective mastitis (Color Plate 7–12) is generally thought to be *Staphylococcus aureus*, although *Escherichia coli*, *Bacteriode* species, and rarely *Mycobacterium tuberculosis* and *Candida albicans* have been cultured.

Bilateral infective mastitis is rare, is generally thought to be group *A streptococci*, and may be life threatening.

 A medical doctor should see patients with bilateral mastitis. Suspected bilateral mastitis is a medical emergency.

 The mother should be instructed to take the full dose of the antibiotic even after symptoms are resolved.

Recurrent mastitis may be related to:

- Anemia

 The mother with unilateral infective mastitis should be treated with antibiotics, encouraged to breastfeed frequently, and care for herself with rest, plenty of fluids, and fever reduction as needed.

- Inadequate or noncompliant use of antibiotics

 Mothers with recurrent mastitis should be examined by a physician for low blood iron.

Fetherston (1998) indicates that unilateral infective mastitis may be related to:

- A cracked nipple (by which the organism can travel into the breast; may cause the mother so much pain that she is reluctant to remove milk from that breast frequently or sufficiently)
- Nipple misshapen after a feeding
- Inadequate milk transfer, hurried feeds, or engorgement
- Infrequent feedings
- Plugged duct that did not resolve properly
- Short frenulum of the infant
- Use of plastic shells, nipple shield, or tea strainers on the breast
- Constricting clothing or tight bra

The mother also reports flu-like symptoms. Her breasts feel hot and are tender. The mother's breasts are reddened.

 Comfort measures for the woman include keeping the milk flowing and the infant nursing as much as possible.

 Mastitis is not a contraindication for breastfeeding

  ## Misplaced nipple pores

Nipple pores are occasionally found in other locations besides the nipple tip, such as along the shank of the nipple, on the areola (may look at first like a Montgomery gland), or rarely on the breast. The ductal system is otherwise normal. Mothers report considerable leaking from these pores.

No visible Montgomery glands, no sign of Montgomery gland secretion

Montgomery glands become more prominent in pregnancy and begin secretion of a glossy fluid that is both lubricating and antimicrobial. Montgomery gland secretion can be seen as one signal that the hormones of pregnancy for lactation are preparing the breasts.

 If the Montgomery glands do not develop and/or there is no glossy sheen on the areola, especially in combination with an atypical vein pattern and lack of increase in breast size, frequent weight checks and close pediatric supervision of the breastfeeding infant is warranted.

Hair on the areola

There is no indication to remove hair growing on the breast or areola. There is a wide variation in the amount of hair, texture, color, etc. Hair on the areola should not impact breastfeeding. Occasionally a hair follicle may become infected. Hair removal on the breast during lactation may open the follicles to a secondary infection.

 Rash on the breast or areola

Rash on the breast is often contact dermatitis (Color Plate 7–13), caused by irritating substances in contact with the skin.

 Although usually caused by local irritants, a health-care provider should closely follow any rash on the breast or areola.

The condition may be painful during feeding, between feedings, or both. Careful questioning of the mother should include asking about possible irritants, such as:

- Creams, salves, lotions, or other preparations she might have applied to the area
- Gadgets (breast pump flanges, shields, shells, and so on) she might have been using, and her cleaning techniques for these items
- Bra pads that contain plastic or leaking devices she may have worn in her bra
- Cleaning techniques used for her bra or washable bra pads
- Changes to her routine that may have precipitated the skin reaction (wearing a bathing suit for hours a day, for example)
- Contagious skin problems on her body or in the family

 Any suspected irritants should be removed from the mother's routine. Infection should be treated.

Common causes of breast and areola rashes include:

- Eczema and atopic dermatitis. Eczema or atopic dermatitis is a red, dry rash wherein the skin flakes off like "oily potato chips." The mother will report a burning or itching type of soreness not related to the actual breastfeeding. Discovery of the irritant and its removal are necessary before the condition will resolve.
- Impetigo—bacterial dermatitis. Impetigo can begin as a concentrated area of redness and progress to itchy vesicles, erosions, and honey-colored crusts.

Impetigo is highly contagious and is spread by contact from the lesions. The mother must seek medical care and be treated. The infant should be checked daily for lesions and treated rapidly, especially if the infant is less than 3 months of age.

- Hives. These very itchy wheals, or raised areas, may be caused by contact with or ingestion of an allergic substance or food. Prescribers may recommend anti-histamines.

- Psoriasis. Psoriasis is a skin disease that first appears as small, red papules topped by fine, silver-white scales. The scales are attached at the center of the lesion and leave a fine bleeding point when detached. Because psoriasis is a chronic disease, it is likely that the mother with psoriasis appearing on her nipple or breast is familiar with the condition. Breastfeeding is not con-traindicated.

- Poison ivy. See previous discussion of this condition.

- *Candida* infection, thrush, or yeast on the nipple or breast (Color Plate 7–14). Although nipple or breast skin affected with an overgrowth of *Candida albicans* may not look any different from nonaffected skin, the mother reports excruciat-ing pain during feedings, between feedings, or both. The mother's nipple and/or areola may appear bright pink or red and the mother might complain of itching in this area.

Diagnosis of yeast of the breast or nipple is often one of exclusion or presumed because the infant has white, yeasty patches in its mouth. The infant's diaper area may also have a skin rash. Laboratory testing is difficult because *Candida* may also live harmlessly on the skin.

Consider possible sources of contamination or vectors such as pacifiers, breast pump parts, towels, and so on.

Other skin conditions

- Tattoos, if present, do not interfere with breastfeeding.

- Dimpling of the breast or areola can be seen alone or in combination with a lump, off-center nipple, and/or peau d'orange (dimples similar to those on an orange peel).

Dimpling or peau d'orange should be examined by a physician immedi-ately. These appearances are associated with breast cancer.

- Moles. Women may have moles on their breasts, as they may have moles on other parts of their body. The moles do not interfere with breastfeeding. Women with moles should consult with their physicians and give themselves a self-skin exam regularly. According to the American Cancer Society, be concerned if moles change suddenly or have the A,B,C,D characteristics:

  ∘ **A** is for asymmetry; one-half of the mole does not match the other half of the mole.

  ∘ **B** is for border; irregular, ragged, notched, or blurred edges.

  ∘ **C** is for color; the pigmentation is not uniform with different shades of brown and black, sometimes with patches of red, white, and blue.

  ∘ **D** is for diameter; greater than 6 millimeters (American Cancer Society, 2001).

Pigmentation alterations

- Hyperpigmentation, or areas of more intense color on the breast, is unrelated to breastfeeding.
- Stretch marks radiating out from the areola may be noted (Color Plate 7–15) Stretch marks are benign and may be seen as yellow, red, bluish, white, or brown streaks on the breast.
- Erosion of the pigmented layer of skin can be the result of a faulty position for breastfeeding. One area of the nipple may have been subjected to repeated trauma such that several layers of skin have been scraped off.

 Observation of the location of the pigment erosion from faulty positioning can provide helpful clues to the positioning problem. Generally, the eroded area has been abraded by inappropriate positions, scraped along the infant's hard palate, or the ridge between the hard and soft palate.

   ## Partial or absent sensation of the areola and nipple

Partial or absent enervation of the nipple or areola may negatively impact the production and delivery of milk. This is especially important to assess if the mother has a history of:

- Surgery, especially breast reduction or augmentation using the periareolar technique
- Trauma to the chest, such as in a car accident
- Placement of a chest tube, especially if the mother herself was born prematurely

 Ask the mother to describe the sensation she feels as she moves her finger around the areola. Can she feel the movement of her finger? Is the sensation equal around the whole areola? Ask the mother if the nipple responds to cold or sexual stimulation by becoming more evert.

 Observe the nipple during a feeding. Does the nipple evert, responding to the infant's lips?

 If there is any question about the enervation of the nipple and/or areola, it is important to provide close pediatric follow-up and frequent weight checks of the infant.

   ## Absence of nipple—Athelia

Mammary tissue without nipple tissue may be found in an accessory breast or in an otherwise normal breast. This is usually a:

- Congenital malformation

  but may also be due to:

- Nipple trauma
- Nipple burn
- Nipple surgery (removed during breast reduction or augmentation but reattachment was not successful)

An enervated nipple with patent ducts is necessary to continued production of milk. Lack of nipple tissue will not affect lactogenesis II (the abundant supply of milk "coming in") but will compromise the continuing production of milk (lactogenesis III).

 **Inverted nipples**

Inverted nipples retract inward (toward the chest wall) when stimulated rather than outward. If the nipples remain inverted during a feeding, the nipple may not be adequately stimulated, resulting in very little prolactin secretion and, thus, little milk production. In research studies of breastfed infants re-admitted to the hospital for breastfeeding malnutrition (failure to thrive) and dehydration, three out of five infants had mothers with inverted nipples (Cooper et al., 1995).

The "pinch test" is often recommended to check to see if inward retracting nipples are truly inverted. The nipple and areola are pressed between the thumb and forefinger. The inverted nipple will retract.

Inverted nipples have been classified into three grades (Han & Hong, 1999):

- Grade 1 inverted nipples—are easily pulled out (by using a breast pump or by the infant nursing well, for example). See the inverted nipples shown in Color Plate 7–16 prior to feeding, and in Color Plate 7–17 immediately after feeding.
- Grade 2 inverted nipples—can be pulled out but don't maintain their projection (most inverted nipples fall into this group).
- Grade 3 inverted nipples—are difficult or impossible to pull out.

Women with inverted nipples before or during pregnancy may find that their nipples evert by the end of pregnancy. The frequency of inverted nipples is not known. The effect on lactation may depend on the degree of inversion. During pregnancy, there is no effective technique to evert the nipples, although a variety of plastic devices and exercises have been recommended. When plastic shells were used, women initiated breastfeeding at a low level as compared to controls and gave up breastfeeding at higher percentages by 6 weeks (Alexander et al., 1992). Postpartum use of these techniques (shells, exercises, everters, and pumps) has not been studied. An infant may nurse well even though the nipple remains inverted in its mouth. The milk supply will decrease over time, however, as the nipple is not adequately stimulated. It has been suggested that inverted nipples have fewer ducts radiating from them. The reason for inverted nipple may be:

- Congenital

 Ask the mother if her nipple has ever everted. Is she able to manipulate it out? Is she able to keep it out during the nursing? Will the nipple come out in response to pumping? If the nipple cannot be documented as everting, frequent weight checks and close pediatric follow-up of the infant are indicated.

- Engorgement or fullness of the breast that obliterates the nipple

 Fullness of the breast and hardness around the nipple may make it difficult for the infant to latch-on as well as for the nipple to evert into the infant's mouth. Fullness may be relieved by hand expressing, or gently pumping or soaking the breasts in a basin of lukewarm water. Gentle massage may also be helpful.

- Cancer of the breast (causing a distortion of the breast and nipple)

 Prompt attention from a diagnostician is required if the breast or nipple is distorted (as shown in Color Plate 7–9) or if any other signs of breast cancer are described. The signs of breast cancer listed by the American Cancer Society (2001) include:

  ○ A new lump or a mass in the breast. A lump that is painless, hard, and has irregular edges is more likely to be cancer. But some cancers are tender, soft, and rounded.

- ° Skin irritation or dimpling.
- ° Nipple pain or the nipple turning inward.
- ° Redness or scaliness of the nipple or breast skin.
- ° A nipple discharge other than breast milk.
- ° A lump in the underarm area.

It is not possible to know how a nipple will function solely by looking at it in its resting state. The assessor must observe a feeding before coming to any conclusion about the possible impact of an unusual nipple presentation on feeding.

Flat nipple

The flat nipple does not protrude away from the areola at rest but everts in response to cold or sexual stimulation. The congenital flat nipple may evert due to changes during pregnancy or in response to active suckling. The flat nipple may be:

- Congenital

 Ask the mother what has caused her nipple to evert in the past. Is she able to manipulate it out? The flat nipple will generally evert appropriately in the infant's mouth during nursing.

- Due to engorgement or fullness of the breast

 It may be difficult for the infant to latch-on to the very full breast. Fullness may be relieved by hand expressing, or gently pumping or soaking the breasts in a basin of lukewarm water. Gentle massage may also be helpful.

- Lack of stimulation

 An infant does not need an everted nipple in order to latch-on to the breast. The occasional infant may find it easier to nurse if the nipple is everted before it begins the nursing session.

- Use of muscle relaxants

 Ask the mother about any drugs or medications she may have been given or may be taking.

Unusually shaped nipples: Bifurcated, club headed, raspberry, long, short, etc.

Although most nipples fit into a similar configuration, occasionally a breastfeeding mother may have an unusually shaped or sized nipple. The etiology of the nipple shape is almost always:

- Congenital. See the raspberry nipple shown in Color Plate 7–18. This nipple functioned normally; however, others that look like this may not function normally.

 The shape of the nipple may not be relevant to the infant's nursing at the breast. Achieving an optimal gape and ensuring that the infant nurses with a wide-open mouth may be helpful.

The shape of the nipple may also be the result of:

- Trauma

 Deep nipple fissures from improper breastfeeding position can permanently bifurcate, or divide, the nipple.

The nipple pores may or may not be patent (open). The nipple may not function in lactation. Close followup to assure patency is recommended.

   ## Fissures or cracked nipples

Fissures are ulcers or crack-like sores on the breast. They usually correspond to areas that have been pinched consistently during nursing or areas of abrasion due to poor positioning. They may be caused by one of the following:

- Trauma to the nipple from incorrect positioning, as shown in Color Plate 7–19.

 Correcting the positioning of the infant during breastfeeding should help stop nipple trauma thereby fostering healing fissures that have been caused by faulty latch-on. If there is also a nipple infection, antibiotic therapy may be necessary.

- Herpes lesions. Breastfeeding is contraindicated while there is a herpes lesion on the breast. See the section Blisters on the breast or areola for more information.

Colostrum and mature milk

  ### Colostrum, transitional milk, and mature milk

From mid-pregnancy until 2–3 days postpartum, the hormones of pregnancy influence the production of colostrum. This is called lactogenesis stage I. Copious milk production normally is seen on the second or third day postpartum in response to the precipitous drop in progesterone that comes from the complete delivery of the placenta (Cregan & Hartmann, 1999).

- Colostrum is thick and creamy and ranges from yellow to yellow-orange in color.
- Transitional milk (day 2–3 through 7–10) is a mixture of colostrum and mature milk.
- Mature milk (usually after day 7–10) is watery, bluish in color, and contains no colostrum. The fat in human milk will float to the top of a container of milk and form a thick, creamy layer.

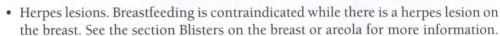 Nonmilk discharges from the nipple should be evaluated. They may be of significance and should be evaluated and diagnosed.

- Unusually colored milk has also been reported. In some cases, the infant's urine is also unusually pigmented. Most of the reports of colored milk attribute the color to pigments in substances the mother has been exposed to in her diet, by medications, and by home remedies such as herbs.
  - Pink or pink-orange milk has been reported after exposure to red and yellow food dyes. Colored urine in the infant has also been reported (Roseman, 1981).
  - Pink, red-brown, or bloody milk (guiaiac positive), also called "rusty pipe" milk, is generally attributed to minor rupture of blood vessels in the breast (see Color Plate 7–20). It may be related to pumping with too high vacuum pressure.

 Blood in milk is always of concern. The mother may not know her milk is bloody until the infant's stool is positive for blood (guiac test for occult blood). Although this is not harmful to the infant, medical evaluation is imperative to rule out pathology.

  - Greenish milk and green-tinged urine in the infant have been associated with the mother drinking green beverages, eating seaweed, or taking tablets of kelp or natural vitamins (Lawrence & Lawrence, 1999).

- ° Black milk has been associated with the mother taking the drug minocycline (Hunt et al., 1996).

- Purulent discharge—Pus may be discharged from the nipple. It is usually yellow or yellow-green in color and is associated with mastitis or abscess. If pus is red, it indicates that small vessels have ruptured.

 Diagnosis and antibiotic therapy are indicated.

White or "blanched nipple"—Raynaud's phenomenon—nipple vasospasm

Raynaud's phenomenon is an episodic ischemia usually noted in the fingers and toes and associated with debilitating pain precipitated by cold. Lawlor-Smith and Lawlor-Smith (1996) have described Raynaud's of the nipples. General discussions of Raynaud's phenomenon do not usually describe symptoms in the nipples.

 Not all nipple vasospasm is considered associated with Raynaud's phenomenon. Raynaud's is associated with symptoms in other extremities and the mother should report a history of Raynaud's prior to breastfeeding.

In general, the symptoms of Raynaud's phenomenon or nipple vasospasm are:

- Debilitating pain associated with the removal of the nipple from the infant's mouth.
- Blanching of the nipple. The nipple is uniformly white when removed from the infant's mouth.
- Biphasic or triphasic color sign. The nipple is observed to change from white to blue to normal color or white to blue to raspberry and back to normal color in minutes after the end of a nursing.

 Medication may be indicated. Mothers should also try to avoid changes of temperature (apply warmth to the nipple as soon as the nursing ends) and avoid smoking. Mothers have reported that fish oil and oil of evening primrose added to their diet has been helpful.

Blanching and biphasic or triphasic color changes with debilitating pain may also be associated with untreated nipple trauma with infection.

 Appropriate treatment involves pharmaceutical therapy, correcting improper positioning that contributes to continued nipple trauma, and palliative care—warmth following nursing, for example.

White blanched lines on the nipple

Lines on the nipple that are associated with the shaping of the nipple by the infant's mouth during nursing indicate poor positioning. The nipple should have the same shape and color after a feeding as before. White lines, such as those shown in Color Plate 7–21, indicating disruption of blood supply to those areas of the nipple during the nursing, are usually precursors to cracks or fissures. Blanching on the end of the nipple usually indicates that the nipple has been wedged along the roof of the infant's mouth during the nursing. Blanched lines along the length of the nipple may indicate that the nipple is being compressed between the gums during the feeding.

Observe the nursing and correct positioning. White lines along the length of the nipple often indicate that the infant is positioned too high in relation to the nipple—if the line is consistent with the position of the infant's lower gum line while nursing, or too low in relation to the nipple if the line is consistent with the position of the infant's upper gum line while nursing.

Loose skin on the breast or nipple

Loose or hanging skin on the breast or nipple may be due to:

- Skin tags

 Skin tags on the nipple may be painful during nursing or not a concern. The physician may remove a tag without interrupting the function of the lactating nipple.

or

- Trauma from an improper nursing position

 If the area also shows signs of infection, refer the mother to a physician for evaluation and possibly antibiotic treatments. Evaluate and correct improper nursing position in order to facilitate healing.

Piercing

Body piercing on the breast or nipple has the potential to interfere with breastfeeding. There are several factors that may impact breastfeeding:

- The size and location of the piercing. If the piercing has cut through ducts in the nipple, milk flow may be blocked and plugged ducts may result. Milk may leak through the piercing.
- The amount of infection the mother may have previously experienced and the severity of any scaring from past infections. Duct and nipple pore patency may be compromised.
- The nipple ring may be located on a part of the breast that goes into the infant's mouth or on the nipple. If this is the case, one concern may be whether the ring is secure or in any danger of coming loose in the infant's mouth. Another concern may be that the ring would take up too much room in the infant's mouth or otherwise interfere with the suckling.

Erosion of skin through suckling—abrasion

Continued improper positioning in the same way may abrade the nipple and erode layers of skin. This damaged area may have lost its pigment and be vulnerable to infection.

 Observe carefully for infection in cases of abrasion. Topical or systemic antibiotic therapy may be indicated.

 Help the mother position the baby at the breast to prevent abrasion and further nipple damage.

Difficulty achieving optimal positioning of the infant at the breast

The mother may be assessed to have difficulty with achieving optimal positioning because of:

- Lack of skill, challenges to dexterity on the part of the mother, especially with multiples, with large breasts, or other challenge
- Neural and/or muscular impairment of the mother, such as a mother with cerebral palsy, post-stroke, carpal tunnel syndrome
- Congenital anomaly, such as the mother who has one arm
- Trauma, such as a mother who has had spinal injury resulting from a car accident
- Medications, such as pain medication that may cause drowsiness

 The goal in working with mothers who are challenged is to ensure the safety of the infant while also optimizing breastfeeding.

⑦ 🗀 (Dx) Vaginal discharge

The mother's report of her vaginal discharge should be consistent with the amount of time elapsed in the postpartum period. The red vaginal discharge that begins after the infant is born normally changes to a brownish discharge and then yellow in a few days. Continuation of a red discharge past the early days is a sign that there may be retained placental fragments.

In addition to signaling that the normal hormonal progression toward lactogenesis II and the production of copious amounts of milk is compromised, continuing red discharge may indicate impending hemorrhage. Further assessment of the mother's condition is imperative.

The rapid drop of progesterone comes from the complete delivery of the placenta initiating lactogenesis II 30 hours to 40 hours later (Cregan & Hartmann, 1999). The rapid drop in progesterone can be inhibited by:

- Retained placental fragments. Prolonged blood-tinged discharge and a delay in the onset of lactogenesis II may be indications of retained placental fragments
- Endocrine condition
- Progesterone containing drugs

⑧ ⑦ 🗀 ① Fatigue

Continuing fatigue in the nursing mother should be investigated. The mother may have anemia. Her inadequate levels of blood iron may be due to:

- Chronic anemia
- Anemia due to excessive peripartum blood loss

 Mothers with inadequate levels of blood iron may complain of fatigue, have problems with problem solving, and be at higher risk for mastitis and recurrent mastitis (Fetherston, 1998). Diagnosis and appropriate therapy are imperative.

Other possible contributors to fatigue include:

- Low thyroid levels
- Other endocrine condition (permanent or temporary)
- Postpartum mood disorder
- Sleep disturbances
- Prescription drugs, alcohol, substance abuse
- Adjustment to the parenting role

Mother does not nurse or remove milk appropriately

Occasionally, a mother professes a desire to breastfeed but seems unwilling to feed the infant—express or pump. The mother may not recognize feeding cues or may misinterpret them, resulting in the chronic underfeeding of the infant. This may be due to:

- Chronic/situational depression
- Substance abuse
- Cognitive dissonance
- Educational deficits such as low reading ability or not able to read the language of available materials
- Mother/infant separation
- Inadequate opportunity for teaching or learning
- Misunderstanding of concepts of lactation
- Inadequate teaching
- Inability to understand
- Impaired ability to understand teaching due to language level or language barriers
  - General
  - Situational (stress, pain, etc.)

 Merely encouraging the mother to feed appropriately or reeducating her about appropriate feeding may be inadequate if the mother is depressed, intoxicated, cognitively impaired, and so on. The safety and adequate feeding of the infant must be the first concern.

 Pain

Breastfeeding should be a pleasurable activity. Mothers should be encouraged to seek help for any pain or discomfort. The mother's sensation during nursing may be assessed on a five-point scale:

5 = Very severe pain
4 = Severe pain
3 = Moderate pain
2 = Minor discomfort
1 = No pain, just tugging

(Healthy Children 2000 Project, 2000)

The mother should also be questioned about when the pain occurs, such as:

- During the entire feeding. This may be indicative of improper latch and/or suckling or a breast or nipple condition.

- At the beginning of the feeding only. This may be indicative of poor positioning that the infant corrects when accommodating the flow of milk after the milk lets down.

- Between feedings. This may be indicative of *Candida,* trauma, infection, and Raynaud's phenomenon, for example.

- Constantly. This may be indicative of trauma, infection, and inadequate drainage.

Nonbreast discomfort related to feeding

On occasion, mothers describe other physical, systemic symptoms associated with breastfeeding. These include:

- Nausea. Nausea associated with feeding is thought to be associated with oxytocin release and nipple vasospasm or Raynaud's phenomenon.

- Headache. Headache associated with feeding is thought to be associated with oxytocin release and nipple vasospasm or Raynaud's phenomenon.

- Migraine. Migraine related to feeding is associated with Raynaud's phenomenon.

 Recurrent and/or severe headaches should be further assessed for appropriate diagnosis.

Women occasionally report psychic discomfort related to feeding. Reported symptoms include:

- Uncomfortable feelings related to the infant at the breast. This may be due to the mother's:
  - Emotional reaction to breastfeeding
  - Lack of confidence in her ability to breastfeed
- Panic/anxiety related to feedings. This may be related to:
  - Postpartum reaction disorder
  - Pre-existing condition in the breastfeeding mother
  - Drugs
  - Physical condition, e.g., thyroid storm

Observation of panic or anxiety in the mother or the mother's report of panic and/or anxiety and/or any symptoms of concern requires prompt evaluation from the appropriate practitioner.

SECTION IV

Artifacts and Documentation

Consideration of Artifacts in the Breastfeeding Assessment

8

Introduction

Artifacts are items that require assessment in addition to the mother, the infant, and the feeding interaction. An artifact is anything that can be examined to learn more about the breastfeeding situation.

An artifact is neither good nor bad itself; it must be understood in the context of the situation. For example, a breast pump may discourage one mother from breastfeeding because it makes her feel like a cow being milked, while the same pump may be seen as a lifeline for another mother. In assessing an artifact, the examiner should ask:

- What artifacts are relevant to this breastfeeding situation?
- What artifacts do I see in the environment?
- What artifacts do I have access to?
- What artifacts should I question the mother about?

The artifact must also be evaluated in context for relevance. For example, the presence of a pacifier in an infant's mouth may be pivotal when slow weight gain or nipple pain are present, but not of immediate relevance to breastfeeding in counseling a mother with a thriving older baby who is seeking advice on how to express milk at work.

Of particular concern is the rise of technology designed to improve breastfeeding. Technology has its place; however, technology should not take the place of skillful assessment and intervention.

Pumps

Pumps (Color Plate 8–1) should be chosen and used in a way that is appropriate for the situation. A pump is not a necessary artifact for many breastfeeding mothers. Assess the reasons behind a pump request coming from the mother. Perhaps she is concerned about milk supply and needs help maximizing her at-breast feedings.

The wide range of pumps available complicates the selection of the appropriate pump. Pumps may be classified according to the **amount of use** expected:

- Occasional use pumps are inexpensive and largely ineffective at building a milk supply, but might be used to express a small amount of milk.
- Casual use pumps are used by a mother when she is away from a nursing infant—at work or school, for example.
- Pumps suitable for a pump-dependent mother are capable of keeping up a milk supply for some time when used appropriately.

Pumps may also be classified by:

- *Personal use.* These pumps are not to be shared between mothers, even with the replacement of some parts.
- *Multiple use.* The manufacturer has provided assurance that the parts of these pumps that could become contaminated are provided individually to each mother.

Pumps can also be considered according to the *source of energy.* The energy source can be:

- Manual. The mother serves as the source of power. These are usually casual use pumps, for personal use only.
- Battery operated. The power of these pumps is not as strong as the electric breast pumps and, therefore, they are usually only indicated for occasional or casual use. These are personal use pumps.
- Electric personal use. These casual use pumps often have an optional car adapter.
- Rental or hospital grade electric. These pumps are indicated for the mother who is separated from her infant (if the mother or infant remains hospitalized), if there are multiples, or if the mother is returning to work or school. Rental grade electric breast pumps may also be used when there are concerns about milk supply.

The use of pumps should always be preceded by a thorough assessment of the breastfeeding situation. There are circumstances wherein mechanical milk expression via hand or pump is the only feasible way to initiate and build a milk supply (e.g., infants who are unable to feed at the breast due to severe defects, illness, or prematurity). Otherwise, pumping should not interrupt or supercede feeding at the breast. Pumping while nursing may maximize the amount of milk collected (Figure 8–1). When a pump is deemed to be an appropriate intervention, the pumping mother should always receive proper instruction and counseling regarding the use and care of the pump.

The yield of milk generated by a pumping mother should *not* be used to measure the mother's milk supply. Most pumps operate solely on suction, or negative pressure, and are thus not performing all of the dimensions of the breastfeeding system. Mothers may be able to pump only a fraction of the milk that an infant would elicit from the breast.

Breast and nipple comfort devices

Breast and nipple comfort devices are products made available with the message of preventing or curing breast problems. Assessment of artifacts should always include questioning the mother about what has been given to her or suggested as aides to breastfeeding. Remember, breastfeeding artifacts must always be considered in context. A

FIGURE 8–1 Pumping while breastfeeding.
Used with permission. © Health Education Associates

breast care cream, when used without correcting the position, may cause the mother to feel as though nothing else can be done for her painful nipples, and then she may abandon breastfeeding. An assortment of these common devices is seen in Color Plate 8–2.

Breast shells

Breast shells are hard domes with a flat or curved back and a place for the nipple to protrude into the dome.

 If breast shells are being worn by a postpartum mother, check for red rings on the areola or breast indicating too much pressure on the breast. This type of pressure is highly related to mastitis (Fetherston, 1998).

Shells have been used:

- By women with sore nipples. These shells have a different back than the shells for inverted nipples. Research indicates they may not be an effective intervention for sore nipples.

- By women with inverted nipples. Historically, breast shells were worn prenatally by women with inverted nipples. This use is no longer suggested (Alexander, et al., 1992). Studies of postpartum use of shells for inverted nipples have not been reported.

Breastfeeding pillows

Pillows may help or hinder breastfeeding. Positioning of pillows may interfere with correct latch-on. Ideally, mothers should position their babies well. Pillows may then be used, if needed, to maintain the position comfortably. Mothers may be observed nursing in poor position because their pillow is too high or too low for their comfort. Pillows are not a necessity for all mothers.

Creams or soothing agents

Any cream or other agent applied to the area of the breast that the infant contacts when feeding must be safe for the infant to ingest. Even small amounts of cream that are wiped off before feeding may be ingested by the infant. When discussing creams with the mother, be specific about:

- The type of cream
- How often the cream is being used
- The amount of cream being used
- Why the mother is using the cream
- How the cream is being used

Research studies have shown that creams are placebos at best. Many products are on the market and suggested for nursing mothers. The cream may be:

- Lanolin-based. Purelan® or Lansinoh® are lanolin-based creams that are thought to be appropriate for use on lactating women. These products have been modified and are hypoallergenic. Lanolin that is hydrous and not modified is highly allergenic.
- Vitamin E. Vitamin E is not recommended for use on breasts due to concerns about ingestion by the infant (Marx, et al., 1985).
- Petroleum jelly. This is not recommended for use on breasts due to concerns about ingestion by the infant.
- Vitamin A & D cream. This cream is for external use only. It is not recommended for use on the breast because the infant might consume it.
- Mammol ointment. This cream contains bismuth substrate, which is thought to be possibly reduced to nitrate by bacteria in the infant's bowel and is a potential cause of methoglobinemia.
- Masse cream. This cream contains peanut oil and other potentially problematic ingredients. Peanut oil can be aspirated and cause bronchitis or can be an allergen.
- Hydrogel and glycerine gel pads. These products are sold to soothe sore nipples. Both have been shown to be safe and effective for moist wound healing elsewhere on the body.
- Other creams and agents. These products, such as bag balm, Eucerin cream, moist towelettes, and antiseptic spray, are used for sore nipples. These items are deemed for external use only and are not recommended for use on the breast of a nursing mother.

Nipple shields

Nipple shields are made of thin silicon or latex. They are worn over the mother's nipple and remain in the infant's mouth when nursing. These shields resemble a sombrero. They have been suggested for use when breastfeeding:

- Premature infants, assisting the infant to transition to the breast (Meier, et al., 2000).
- Full-term infants. No clinical evidence supports their use for full-term infants. Nipple shields can interfere with milk production and the infant can become accustomed to nursing with a nipple shield.

 In the report of successful use of nipple shields with preterm infants, the mothers were pump dependent for their ongoing milk supply.

Infant feeding devices

Infant feeding devices have been recovered from archaeological sites of many civilizations. The ones currently used may be characterized as either "at-breast" feeders from which the baby receives nourishment from the device while also breastfeeding or as feeders such as bottles, cups, spoons, etc. with which the baby is fed away from the breast. Commonly available devices are pictured in Color Plate 8–3.

"At breast" feeding systems

"At breast" feeders consist of a container to hold the breast milk or formula, joined to tubing lying along the nipple. While the infant suckles at the breast, the tubing delivers additional fluid, as seen in Figure 8–2. Systems include:

- Lact-Aid®: A closed system, consisting of a thin tube attached to a cap and plastic disposable bag. The Lact-Aid hangs around the mother's neck with the tube extending to the nipple. Originally designed for adopted infants, this device is also used by women who wish to supplement while nursing. Formulas made from powder and meat are not to be used with the Lact-Aid.

- Supplemental Nutritional System®: A feeding tube system in which two tubes are attached to a plastic container that holds breastmilk or formula. The mother wears the system hanging from her neck with one tube extending to each nipple. As the infant feeds from one side, the tubing of the opposite breast can be closed off to prevent leaking. Formulas made from powder and meat do not flow well through the tubing. A short-term use system with one tube is also available.

Bottles and artificial nipples

Concerns with bottles and artificial nipples interfering with successful breastfeeding have led UNICEF and WHO to include strong statements against their use. Concerns include:

- The breastfed infant may prefer the bottle.
- Infants may develop a preference for a particular bottle nipple.
- Bottles and nipples are hard to clean properly.

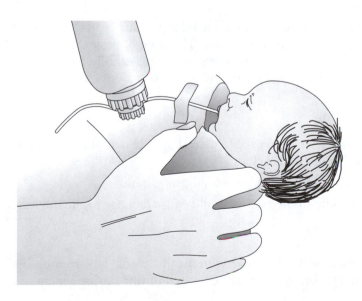

FIGURE 8–2 At-breast supplementation.

Used with permission. © Health Education Associates

- Mothers who are exposed to bottles in the postpartum report that their nipples are more painful.
- Bottles are a popular symbol for infants, leading people to believe that bottles are the normal infant feeding method.

Cups

Using open cups is a safe, alternative feeding method when feeding at the breast is not possible (Howard et al., 1999b). However:

- The cup must be food- or medical-grade.
- Infants may become habituated to the cup.
- The parents need to understand that the method of feeding an infant via a cup is different from their own use of a cup. Infants can aspirate fluid if cup feeding is not performed skillfully.

Finger-feeding device

This artifact is used with the intention of adding nutrition to infants who are having difficulty maintaining a correct suck or latch or with infants who refuse the breast. The mother places a tube on her finger (the finger that is closest in size to her nipple) and the finger is drawn into the infant's mouth. Breastmilk or formula is placed in the container attached to the tube. (Reconstituted powdered formula and meat-based formula should be avoided because they do not flow easily through the tubing.) There are some concerns about this method of supplementation:

- Infants can become addicted to this type of feeding and weaning them to the breast can be difficult.
- Some healthcare professionals consider the placement of a finger inside the infant's mouth to be an invasive procedure and are reluctant to implement this method.
- Some infants have had oral aversion after being fed this way.

    There is no published research to support the use of finger feeding.

Gavage tube

Gavage tubes are feeding devices used for infants (usually in the neonatal intensive care unit) who are unable to feed orally. The tube is passed through the nose or mouth into the stomach or the small intestine. Breast milk, formula, or other prescribed fluids are administered via the tube.

Periodontal syringe

Periodontal syringes have been used to deliver supplementation to breastfed infants. Concerns about this method include:

- The syringe was not designed as a food-grade item.
- The sharp opening of the syringe could cause damage to the infant's oral cavity.

Syringe

In some instances, a medical syringe without the needle has been used to deliver a feeding supplementation to an infant. Presence of this device generally means that a healthcare provider has given it to a mother to supplement an infant with a questionable weight gain. These syringes may be used as an at-breast supplementer, or a finger-feeding device. Syringes are difficult to clean and may pose risks if reused.

Pacifiers

Pacifier use is associated with an increased risk of ear infections and recurrent ear infections in research studies (Niemela, 1995). Pacifiers may be used with:

- Preterm infants. Pacifiers may be indicated for use in the special care nursery. Sucking on a pacifier in preterm infants may improve growth.
- Full-term infants. There are concerns about use of pacifiers in full-term infants. Pacifier use may decrease breastfeeding duration, as feedings may be missed and mothers may use them in place of getting help with sore nipples (Howard, 1999a; Righard, et al., 1997).

 If the assessor notes a pacifier in the environment, further questions should include:

- Is the mother scheduling feedings and using a pacifier to stall the infant?
- Does the mother have sore or painful nipples? Is she using the pacifier to decrease the time of feedings?
- Is the infant difficult to soothe without a pacifier?

Written documents

Written documents are artifacts that may be generated by the assessor, healthcare provider, mother, or community. These may include:

- Care plans for breastfeeding
- Telephone counseling documentation
- Referral forms from other providers
- Laboratory reports
- Medical records
- Assessment documents
- Infant growth records
- Educational pamphlets on breastfeeding management
- Community resource list

These written documents should be reviewed by the assessor and taken into consideration with respect to the context of the mother's and infant's breastfeeding experience.

Breastfeeding assessment tools

A variety of assessment tools have been developed. Validity, interrater, and intrarater reliability have not been demonstrated for many of these tools (Riordan & Koehn, 1997). Tools in use include:

- LATCH (Jensen et al., 1994)
- IBFAT (Infant Breast Feeding Assessment Tool) (Matthews, 1988)

- MBA (Mother Infant Assessment for Breastfeeding) (Mulford, 1992)
- SAIB (Systematic Assessment of the Infant at Breast) (Shrago & Bocar, 1990)
- LAT (Lactation Assessment and Corrective Intervention Tool) (Healthy Children 2000 Project, Inc., 2000)

Other resources for assessors

Childbirth Graphics—1-800-299-3366 X287—www.childbirthgraphics.com

- Rapid Assessment Form
- Care Plan Forms (general and special situations)

Healthy Children 2000 Inc.—(508) 888-8044—www.healthychildren.cc

- Training programs:
  - Maternal & Infant Assessment for the Lactation Consultant

Health Education Associates—888-888-8077—www.aboutus.com/a100/healthed

- Documentation/guidance forms:
  - Anticipatory Guidance Documentation Form
  - Comprehensive Risk Assessment Tool for Breastfed Babies
  - Feeding Cues for Breastfed Babies & Mother's Log
  - Infant Growth Charts for Breastfed Girls & Boys
  - Postpartum Assessment Tool for Breastfed Babies
- Digital scales with breastmilk intake function
- Video: *Breasts & Breastfeeding: Common Early Concerns*

Lactation Institute—818-995-1913—www.lactationinstitute.org

- Lactation charting forms:
  - Phone History
  - Intake Form
  - Case Log Form
  - Maternal/Infant History
  - Notes
  - Breast and Infant Physical Assessment for Lactation
  - Instructions to Mother
  - Mother and Baby's Daily Log
- Educational slide series—More than 400 slides regarding breastfeeding and human lactation

Creating Documentation

9

Introduction

Documentation and record keeping are important skills for those who care for lactating mothers and infants. The records should:

- Be complete
- Be clearly written
- Be concise
- Provide the assessor with a quick review to access during follow-up contacts with the mother and infant
- Facilitate easy sharing of assessment findings with other healthcare providers for the continuity of care for the mother and infant
- Allow assessors to research their own databank of similar cases, in order to review possible contributing factors and the success of strategies applied

 All records produced in the course of breastfeeding assessment are legal evidence of professional accountability. In case of malpractice claims, a complete and clear record provides solid evidence of the interaction with the mother and infant. Without documentation, interactions with mother and infant are assumed not to have occurred.

Documentation provides a means for continuous quality assurance/quality improvement.

The basic rules of record keeping

Assessors should assure that basic rules of record keeping are observed. These rules include:

- Record all interactions, however brief, with a mother and infant.
- Use permanent ink pen (not pencil) to record all notes.
- Correct any errors made in the process of writing the record only by drawing a single line through errors. The line should be initialed and dated to protect

against appearance of alteration of the record at a later date. Correction fluid and cover-up tape should never be used in counseling records. Errors discovered after the time of the interaction should not be corrected in the original record, but noted in the follow-up notes.

- Avoid use of excessive abbreviation and acronyms. If used, the record should contain a "key" to decoding the abbreviations and acronyms used.

- Record notes during the counseling session and write summaries as soon as possible after the session to preserve the integrity of the interaction.

- Date and sign all records.

- Keep original records for 7 years or longer. Assessors should consult with national and state law authorities to determine how long to retain records.

Obtain consent before the interaction

Before interacting with any mother and infant, the assessor should obtain the mother's consent verbally and in writing. The consent form should include:

- Information about the expected content of the assessment, for example:
  - Observing the mother and infant breastfeeding
  - Assessing the mother and the infant
  - Weighing and measuring of the infant
- Indication of the mother's consent to share assessment findings and treatment plans with the mother's and infant's healthcare providers

 There are several legal and ethical issues related to informed consent. It is recommended that assessors seek information and counsel regarding these issues. An excellent resource is P. G. Bornmann (2002). *A legal primer for lactation consultants,* in M. Walker, ed. (2002). *Core curriculum for lactation consultant practice.* Sudbury: Jones & Bartlett Publishers.

Note taking during the interaction

Throughout all interactions with mothers, assessors should:

- Record succinct notes
- Identify significant findings
- Identify key elements of the care plan

 Documentation of these findings and the plan is essential to professional practice.

 Depending on the custom of the assessor's employer, specific documentation forms may be required or assessors may be able to purchase, adapt, or develop lactation documentation forms.

Intake information

The scope of practice ranges widely among breastfeeding assessors, including nurses, nutritionists, social workers, peer counselors, physicians, occupational therapists, etc. For this reason, the type of assessment data and key data recorded will range widely among individual assessors.

Intake data collected should always include the following:

- Name of mother
- Reason for consultation
- Mother's mailing and street address
- Mother's home and business telephone number
- Name of and contact information for mother's obstetric care provider
- Infant's name
- Infant's date of birth
- Infant's birth weight
- Name and contact information for infant's pediatric care provider
- Source of referral
- Other information should be collected as necessary (e.g., insurance information if the assessor is billing insurance for lactation care)

History

Eliciting information of the mother's and infant's history is a crucial part of the assessment.

Maternal history can include pertinent information regarding:

- Postpartum period
- Labor and delivery
- Pregnancy and pre-pregnancy periods of the mother's life

The maternal history may also include previous pregnancies, labors, deliveries, and breastfeeding experiences.

Infant history can include pertinent information from:

- Fetal development
- Labor and delivery
- Postpartum periods

In gathering historical information, the assessor is searching for facts that can impact the current breastfeeding situation.

Assessment for breastfeeding performed during the prenatal period should include careful history taking (Powers & Slusser, 1997). Ask about:

- Feeding decision and previous feeding choices
- Previous postpartum hemorrhage, chest or breast surgery, breast trauma
- Breast changes during pregnancy
- Family history of breast cancer
- Maternal concerns about breasts and/or breastfeeding
- Examination of the breasts
- Communication of any concerns to other caregivers
- Inclusion of mother's partner and/or other pertinent family members in discussions
- Assessment of mother's awareness of professional and community support systems

Postpartum history could include the following additions:

- How are you feeling now?
- How was your pregnancy?
- Did you have difficulty conceiving?
- Any hormonal problems (thyroid, diabetes, etc.)? Are you currently taking any medications? Smoking? Drinking alcohol?
- Would you tell me about your labor and delivery experience with this baby (include pain relief methods used, procedures, etc.)?
- What happened immediately after the birth (procedures performed, skin-to-skin, vaginal bleeding, etc.)?
- What were the first feedings like?
- How are feedings going now?
- How do you know when it is time to feed the baby?
- How do feedings end?
- When did feeding difficulties begin?
- What do you think caused/causes these difficulties?
- When do the difficulties occur? Always? At a specific time of day, environment, infant state, etc.?
- What have you tried to improve the situation (pacifiers, pumps, other gadgets, other feeding strategies, etc.)?
- Would you "walk me through" the last 24 hours and tell me about your feeding and caring interactions with your baby?
- What are your goals regarding breastfeeding?

Lab reports

Relevant laboratory reports include results of medically ordered laboratory tests of physiologic conditions that could impact the breastfeeding situation. Examples of pertinent laboratory test might include infant plasma bilirubin levels, mother's hematocrit, infant's blood glucose levels, and so on.

Key components of documentation

The important components of documentation during and after the assessment should include:

- Clear, concise notes taken during the course of the interaction with mother and infant. Items should include:
  - Notation of mother's reason for visit
  - Record of mother's and infant's history
  - Notes of observation of mother/infant interaction, including feeding
  - Notation of any measurements made or observed during visit, including weight, length, head circumference, ounces of milk expressed, formula given, etc.

- ○ Record of all quantitative measurements made or noted during the visit (e.g., infant weight, volume of milk expressed, etc.)

- ○ Notation of all activities performed (weighing, observing feeding, demonstrating altered positions, etc.) and all products used or suggested during the consultation (supplemental feeders, pumps, etc.)

- A summary tool (such as a pre-printed report form, or use of SOAP and PIE notes, described later)

- Summary of instructions/suggestions made to mother or a photocopy or carbon copy of the actual instructions

- Indication of the follow-up plan, including planned telephone or meeting arrangements. Answering the following questions is helpful:

  - ○ How soon is follow-up planned?

  - ○ Who will contact whom?

  - ○ What format will the follow-up take? Telephone? Visit?

- Indication of any referrals made by the assessor

Assessment and care-planning documentation

Several formats for assessment and care-planning documentation, including SOAP notes and PIE notes, are utilized in the health professions.

SOAP notes

The SOAP note was developed in the Problem Oriented Medical Record (POMR) system of data analysis and patient care planning and is used in many healthcare settings. The POMR begins with a collection of a database of information gathered through patient health history, then records each subsequent "problem" in SOAP note formation. The acronym SOAP denotes:

S Subjective data. The situation or problem as stated in the mother's words. Many assessors record the mother's words verbatim in quotations.

O Objective data. Indication of any objective findings of the interaction: the infant's weight, length, pre- and post-feed weights, ounces of milk expressed by mother during the interaction, etc.

A Assessment. The assessor's assessment of the situation or problem

P Plan. The care plan as agreed to by assessor and mother, as well as any referrals made and plans for follow-up

Some healthcare systems use the acronym SOAPER, adding the following components to SOAP:

E Education. Special instructions, pamphlets, etc. given

R Return. When and under what circumstances to return to assessor

Other healthcare agencies use the acronym SOAPIER, adding the following to SOAP:

I Intervention. What was actually done

E Evaluation. Review and outcomes of the assessment, plan, and intervention

R Re-evaluation. Follow-up evaluation after a certain amount of time

Sample documentation using SOAP notation

A sample SOAP note recording a lactation counseling session:

Mother: Jane Doe   *Mother's Contact & Mailing Information:*

Infant: John Doe   *Date of Birth:* June 18, 2001   *Current Age:* 2 weeks, 2 days

Location of Visit: LC Office   *Time of Visit:* 10:15 a.m.–12:00 p.m.

S:

Mother states: "My infant has only wanted to nurse on my right breast since birth. That breast is making more milk. I don't think this is normal. My infant is gaining weight fine. I called my midwife about this and she said I should come and see you." Mother reports normal, uneventful pregnancy; "Ok" 12-hour labor, unmedicated, normal birth. First pediatric visit scheduled for 7/6/01. Mother reports 6–8 feeds q. 24 hrs. "Waiting for him to root to start feeds."

O:

Data recorded from infant immunization record: Birth weight 7 pounds, 3 ounces; Hospital discharge weight 6 pounds, 12 ounces

Data recorded today:

Anthropometric: 7 pounds, 6 ounces—weight gain +3 ounces from birthweight, +10 ounces from discharge weight. Lowest weight unknown.

Visual: Marked discrepancy between mother's breast sizes is visually evident: left breast smaller than the right. More visible veins in right breast.

Feeding observation: Infant appeared active, not noticeably jaundiced. Suckling was sustained for 5 minutes on left breast, 13 minutes on right. Positioning at the breast was adequate, but not optimal. Pre- and post-feed weights show no measurable milk transfer on left breast, 2 ounces of milk transferred on right breast.

A:

1. ? Milk insufficiency: Infant needs immediate pediatric follow-up to determine weight status and assess need for supplementation.

2. Weight gain marginal.

3. Additional milk expression may be required to increase milk supply; a milk expression plan was recommended.

4. Positioning and latch-on need improvement—deeper latch achieved during consult.

P:

1. Get weight checked on pediatrician's scale immediately. Appointment scheduled for 3:00 p.m. today.

2. Keep infant skin-to-skin and continue to observe infant for feeding cues, as shown. Goal of 10–12 feeds every 24 hours. Consider using feeding log to keep track.

3. Use loaner digital scale to determine milk transfer during three feedings today and three tomorrow.

4. If less than 2.5 ounces of milk are transferred in a feed, pump after the feed for 5–7 minutes per side, starting on the right, switching to the left for 5 min-

utes, then back to the right for 5 minutes. Feed expressed milk to the baby if supplementation is recommended by a physician or store expressed milk in refrigerator for 48 hours or in freezer for a longer time period.

5. Continue improved positioning and latch, as shown.

6. Call LC later today to report physician's findings and schedule a follow-up consult. Continue to call LC, pedi, and midwife whenever questions arise.

Date of Visit: 7/5/01   Signature: Lactation Consultant

PIE format notes

PIE is an acronym for problem-intervention-evaluation. The PIE format differs from the SOAP format in that the narrative does not include assessment information. Special flowcharts are used to record assessment data. The acronym PIE denotes:

P   Problems applicable to client

I   Interventions or action taken

E   Evaluation of the outcomes of interventions applied and the client's response to the interventions

Sample documentation using PIE format

P:
- Minimal infant weight gain due to insufficient feeding practices and possible insufficient milk supply.

I:
- Assisted client to position infant during latch-on process. Discussed with the mother frequency of feedings and impact on milk supply.
- Encouraged mother to continue to watch for feeding cues with goal to increase feedings to 10–12 per 24 hours.
- Instructed mother to contact pediatrician for weight check and assessment.
- Loaned mother digital scale to perform pre- and post-feed weights ×3 today and tomorrow.
- Instructed mother to pump after any feed in which less than 2.5 ounces of milk is transferred. Pumping routine recommended consisted of 5–7 minutes of pumping on the right breast, switching to 5–7 minutes on the left breast, and then returning to 5–7 minutes on the right breast. Instructed mother to store breastmilk in the refrigerator for 48 hours or in the freezer if milk is to be kept longer.
- Encouraged mother to call LC with results from pediatric appointment and to schedule follow-up visit.

E:
- Infant was successful in achieving a deeper latch, taking in more breast tissue as he nursed.
- Mother verbalized understanding of relationship to increased feeding and increased milk supply.
- Mother agreed to continue watching for feeding cues as signal to feed infant and will attempt to reach goal of 10–12 feedings per 24 hours.

- Appointment scheduled for pediatric visit today at 3:00.
- Mother verbalized understanding of how and when to use digital scale.
- Mother verbalized understanding of how and when to use a breast pump.
- Mother verbalized understanding of milk storage instructions.
- Mother agreed to call LC with results from visit to pediatrician and to schedule follow-up visit with LC.

Assessment information regarding feeding observation, breast observation, infant's weight, and so on would be documented on a separate form.

Follow up and Progress Notes

Follow up and progress notes should be made in similar format (SOAP or PIE) to the original assessment format. All follow up contacts should be briefly, but thoroughly, recorded.

Breastfeeding consultation reports to other healthcare providers

When breastfeeding assessment interactions occur outside the hospital, birth center, or office of a healthcare provider (pediatrician, obstetrician, family practitioner, or midwife), the assessor should send a report summarizing the interaction to the pertinent healthcare provider within 24 hours. It is essential that written maternal consent and permission to release records have been obtained during the interaction.

Sample format of a report to health care provider

LC Practice

Address

Phone & Fax

Breastfeeding Assessment Report

Healthcare Provider Report

    To: *Dr. Pediatrician*

           Nurse-Midwife

    From: *LC*

    Date: 5 July 2001

    Re: Infant *John Doe, d/o/b 6/18/01*

           Mother *Jane Doe, d/o/b 12/6/75*

Subjective:

Her midwife referred Jane Doe, mother of infant John, regarding her breastfeeding concerns. At initial contact today, 7/5/01, Ms. Doe had questions about the normalcy of one-sided breast preference for the infant, reporting that her right breast was secreting much more milk than the other. She reported that her infant was gaining weight appropriately.

Objective:

- *Anthropometric:* 7 pounds, 6 ounces today—a weight gain of +3 ounces from birth weight, +10 ounces from discharge weight at 2 weeks, 2 days of age. Lowest weight unknown.

- *Visual:* Marked discrepancy between mother's breast sizes is visually evident: left breast smaller than the right. More visible veins in right breast.

- *Feeding observation:* Infant appeared active, not noticeably jaundiced, and was able to sustain suckling for several minutes. Positioning at the breast was adequate, but not optimal. Pre- and post-feed weights using a digital scale with milk intake function showed no measurable milk transfer on left breast, 2 ounces of milk transferred on right breast. (NB: Neither measurement is indicative of milk supply, as one test weight cannot determine the adequacy of mother's milk supply.)

Assessment:

1. Milk insufficiency: Infant needs immediate pediatric follow-up to determine weight status and assess need for supplementation.

2. If inadequate milk supply is diagnosed, mother may wish to initiate pumping to increase supply.

3. Positioning and latch-on need improvement.

Plan:

1. Same-day pediatric visit scheduled for 3:00 p.m. today.

2. Digital scale was loaned to mother to track milk intake at the breast over the next several days.

3. Pumping regime was suggested: Pump as often as possible for 5–7 minutes per side, starting on the right, switching to the left for 5 minutes, then back to the right for 5 minutes. Stored milk may be used to supplement infant, if needed.

4. Improvements to positioning and latch were demonstrated, including allowing more head extension so infant can grasp more of the breast tissue, were recommended.

5. Mother was encouraged to contact Center, pediatrician, and midwife as needed for further information or assessment.

Please contact me if I can provide further information.

LC signature   *Date*

References

Alexander, J. M. et al. (1992). Randomized control trial of breast shells: Hoffman's exercises. *British Medical Journal, 304,* 1030.

American Academy of Pediatrics. (1997). Breastfeeding and the use of human milk. *Pediatrics, 100*(6), 1035.

American Cancer Society. (2001). Signs and symptoms of breast cancer. *http://www.cancer.org/eprise/main/docroot/CR.../CRI_2_6X_Benign_Breast_Conditions_5,* downloaded 6/16/2001.

Ardran, G. M., & Kemp, F. H. (1959). A correlation between sucking pressure and the movements of the tongue. *Acta paediatrica Scandinavica, 48,* 261.

Ardran, G. M. et al. (1958). A cinemaradiographic study of breastfeeding. *British Journal of radiology, 31,* 156.

Auerbach, L. (1888). Zur mechanik des saugens und der inspiration. *Archiv fur Physiologie, 59,* 58.

Auerbach, K., & Riordan, J. (2000). *Clinical lactation: A visual guide.* Sudbury, MA: Jones and Bartlett Publishers.

Ballard, J. L. et al. (1991). New Ballard score, expanded to include extremely premature infants. *Journal of pediatrics, 119*(3), 418.

Bates, B. (1995). *A pocket guide to physical examination and history taking.* (2nd ed.). Philadelphia: Lippincott Co.

Biancuzzo, M. (1999). *Breastfeeding the newborn: Clinical strategies for nurses.* St. Louis, MO: Mosby.

Bosma, J. F. et al. (1997). Ultrasound demonstration of tongue motions during suckle feeding. *Developmental medicine and child neurology, 32,* 223.

Bovey, A. et al. (1999). Orofacial exercises for babies with breastfeeding problems. *Breastfeeding review, 7,* 1, 23.

Brazelton, T. (1992). *Touchpoints: Your child's emotional and behavioral development.* Reading, MA: Addison-Wesley.

Brazelton, T. (1995). *Clinics in developmental medicine.* (3rd ed.). London: MacKeith Press.

Brodribb, W. (1997). *Breastfeeding management in Australia.* East Malvern, Australia: Merrily Merrily Enterprises Pty Ltd.

Butte, N. et al. (1991). Heart rates of breast-fed and formula-fed infants. *Journal of pediatric gastroenterology and nutrition, 13,* 391.

Cadwell, K. et al. (2001). Sore nipples in breastfeeding women: A clinical trial of three treatment modalities. *In press.*

Cafarella, J. (Ed.). (1996). *Breastfeeding. . .naturally.* Mitcham, Victoria, Australia: Merrily, Merrily Enterprises Ltd.

Case-Smith, J. (1988). An efficacy study of occupational therapy with high-risk neonates. *American Journal of occupational therapy, 42* (8), 499.

Centuouri, S. et al. (1999). Nipple care, sore nipples and breastfeeding: A randomized trial. *Journal of Human Lactation, 15* (2), 125.

Chan, G. (Ed). (1997). *Lactation: The breast-feeding manual for health professionals.* Chicago: Precept Press.

Chess, S., & Thomas, A. (1999). Dynamics of individual behavioral development. In M. D. Levine et al. (Eds.), *Developmental and behavioral pediatrics.* Philadelphia, PA: W. B. Saunders.

Christensson, K. et al. (1995). Separation distress call in the human neonate in the absence of maternal body contact. *Acta Paediatrica, 84,* 468.

Clark, N. (1985). The study of four methods of nipple care offered to post partum mothers. *New Zealand nursing journal, 78*(6), 16.

Cooper, W. O. et al. (1996). Increased incidence of severe breast-feeding malnutrition and hypernatremia in a metropolitan area. *Pediatrics,* Nov. 1995, 96(5 Pt 1), 957–60.

Cregan, M. D., & Hartmann, P. E. (1999). Computerized breast measurements from conception to weaning: clinical implications. *Journal of human lactation, 15*(2), 89.

Creger, P. (1992). Developmental support in the NICU. In J. Beachy et al. (Eds.), *Core curriculum for neonatal intensive care nursing.* Philadelphia, PA: W. B. Saunders.

Cunningham, A., D. Jelliffe, E. F., and Jelliffe, P. (1992). *Breastfeeding, growth and illness: An annotated bibliography.* New York: UNICEF.

Dana, N., & Price, A. (1985). *Successful breastfeeding: A practical guide for nursing mothers.* New York: Simon and Schuster.

De Carvalho, M. et al. (1982). Milk intake and frequency of feeding in breastfeeding infants. *Early human development, 7,* 575.

De Carvalho, M., et al. (1983). Effect of frequent breastfeeding on early milk production and infant weight gain. *Pediatrics, 72*(3), 307.

Dubowitz, L. M. S. et al. (1970). Clinical assessment of gestational age in newborn infant. *Journal of pediatrics, 77*(1), 4.

Duncan, B. et al. (1993). Exclusive breastfeeding for at least 4 months protects against otitis media. *Pediatrics, 91*(5), 867.

Eiger, M., & Olds, S. (1987). *The complete book of breastfeeding.* New York: Workman.

Fadavi, S. et al. (1997). Mechanics and energetics of nutritive sucking: A functional comparison of commercially available nipples. *Journal of pediatrics, 130,* 740.

Fetherston, C. (1998). Risk factors for lactation mastitis. *Journal of human lactation, 14*(2), 101.

Fildes, V. (1986). *Breasts, bottles and babies: A history of infant feeding.* Edinburgh, Scotland: Edinburgh University Press.

Frank, A. L. et al. (1982). Breast-feeding and respiratory virus infection. *Pediatrics, 70* (2), 239.

Frappier, P. et al. (1987). Nursing assessment of infant feeding problems. *Journal of pediatric nursing,* 2(1), 37.

Glass, R. P., & L. S. Wolf. (1994). Incoordination of sucking, swallowing and breathing as an etiology of breastfeeding difficulty. *Journal of human lactation, 10,* 185.

Goldsmith, H. (1974). Milk rejection sign of breast cancer. *American journal of surgery, 128,* 280.

Gomez, L. T. (1999). Breastfeeding: Increasing primary adjustment milk supply. *International journal of childbirth education, 15* (1), 29.

Graffy, J. P. (1992). Mother's attitudes to and experience of breast-feeding: A primary care study. *British journal of general practice, 42,* 61.

Gunther, M. (1945). Sore nipples causes and prevention. *Lancet, 2,* 590.

Halverson, H. M. (1938). Infant sucking and tensional behavior. *Journal of genetic psychology, 53,* 365.

Halverson, H. M. (1942). The serial organization of sucking in the young infant. *Journal of genetic psychology, 57,* 943.

Hammermen, C. & Kaplan, M. (1995). Oxygen saturation during and after feeding in healthy term infants. *Biology of the neonate, 67,* 94.

Han, S., & Hong, Y. G. (1999). The inverted nipple: Its grading and surgical correction. *Plastic and reconstructive surgery, 104*(2), 389.

Hayashi, Y. et al. (1997). Ultrasonographic analysis of sucking behavior in newborn infants: The driving force of sucking pressure. *Early Human Development, 49,* 33.

Health and Human Services. (2000). *HHS blueprint for action on breastfeeding.* Washington, DC: Author.

Healthy Children 2000 Project. (2000). *The lactation counselor certificate training program: Training curriculum.* Sandwich, MA: Author.

Healthy Children 2000 Project. (2000). *Latch-on assessment tool (LAT).* Sandwich, MA: Author.

Heinig, M., & Dewey, K. (1997). Health effects of breastfeeding for mothers, a critical review. *Nutrition Research Reviews, 10,* 35.

Hewat, R. J., & Ellis, D. J. (1987). A comparison of the effectiveness of two methods of nipple cares. *Birth, 14*(1), 41.

Hill, P., & Humenick, S. (1993). Nipple pain during breastfeeding: The first two weeks and beyond. *The journal of perinatal education, 2*(2), 21.

Hoover, H. (1990). Breast cancer during pregnancy and lactation. *The surgical clinics of North America, 70,* 1151.

Hoover, K. (2001). *The link between infants' oral thrush and nipple and breast pain in lactating women.* (4th ed.). Morton, PA: Author.

Howard, C. R. et al. (1999a). The effects of early pacifier use on breastfeeding duration. *Pediatrics, 103* (3), E 33.

Howard, C. R. et al. (1999b). Physiologic stability of newborns during cup- and bottle-feeding. *Pediatrics, 104*(5), 1204.

Huggins, K. (1986). *The nursing mother's companion.* Boston: The Harvard Common Press.

Huggins, K. et al. (2000). Markers of lactation insufficiency: A study of 34 mothers. *Current issues in Clinical Lactation, 2000,* 25.

Hunt, M. J. et al. (1996). Black breast milk due to minocycline therapy. *Br J Dermatol, 134,* 943.

Ingram, J. C. et al. (1999). Maternal predictors of early breast milk output. *Acta paediatrica, 88*(5), 493.

Jensen, D. et al. (1994). LATCH: A breastfeeding charting system and documentation tool. *Journal of Obstetrics, Gynecology and neonatal nursing, 23*(1), 27.

Jensen, R. G. (1999). Lipids in human milk. *Lipids, 34*(12), 1243.

Jolley, S. (1990). *The breastfeeding triage tool.* Seattle, WA: Department of Public Health, Seattle-King County.

Karpen, M. et al. (1995). *Essentials of maternal-child nursing.* South Easton, MA: Western Schools.

Kashara, M. (1916). The curved lines of suction. *American journal of diseases of children, 1916,* 73.

King E. B., & Goodson, W. H. , III. (1991). Discharges amid secretions of the nipple. In K. I. Cland, & E. M. Copeland (Eds.). *The breast: Comprehensive management of benign and malignant diseases.* Philadelphia, PA: W. B. Saunders.

Kitzinger, S. (1979). *The experience of breastfeeding.* New York: Penguin Books.

Kitzinger, S. (1989). *Breastfeeding your baby.* New York: Alfred A. Knopf.

La Leche League International. (1997). *The womanly art of breastfeeding.* Schaumburg, IL: Author.

Lauwers, J., & Shinskie, D. (2000). *Counseling the nursing mother: A lactation consultant's guide.* (3rd ed.). Sudbury, MA: Jones and Bartlett.

Lawlor-Smith, L. S., & Lawlor-Smith, C. L. (1996). Raynaud's phenomenon of the nipple: A preventable cause of breastfeeding failure. *Med J Aust, 166,* 448.

Lawrence, R., & Lawrence, R. (1999). *Breastfeeding: A guide for the medical profession.* (5th ed.). St. Louis, MO: Mosby.

Livingstone, V., & Stringer, J. S. (1999). The treatment of *Staphylococcus aureus* infected sore nipples: A randomized comparative study. *Journal of human lactation, 15*(3), 241.

Marmet, C., & Shell, E. (1984). Training neonates to suck correctly. *MCN, The American journal of maternal child nursing, 9* (6), 401.

Marmet, C., & Shell, E. (1993). *Lactation forms: A guide to lactation consultant charting.* Encino, CA: Lactation Institute.

Marx, C. et al. (1985). Vit E concentrations in serum of newborn infants and topical use. *American journal of obstetrics and gynecology, 152*:668.

Mathew, O, & Bhatia, J. (1989). Sucking and breathing patterns during breast and bottle-feeding in term neonates. *American journal of diseases of children, 143,* 588.

Matthews, M. K. (1988). Developing an instrument to assess infant breastfeeding behavior in the early neonatal period. *Midwifery, 4*(4), 154.

Matthiesen, A. S. et al. (2001). Postpartum maternal oxytocin release by newborns: Effects of infant hand massage and sucking. *Birth, 28*(1), 13.

McBride, M. C., & Danner, S. C. (1987). Sucking disorders in neurologically impaired infants: Assessment and facilitation of breastfeeding. *Clinics in perinatology, 14*:1, 109.

McGowan, J. S. et al. (1991). Developmental patterns of normal nutritive sucking in infants. *Developmental medicine and child neurology, 33,* 891.

Medoff-Cooper, B. (1991). Changes in nutritive sucking patterns with increasing gestational age. *Nursing research, 40*(4), 245.

Medoff-Cooper, B. , & Gennaro, S. (1996). The correlation of sucking behaviors and Bayley Scales of Infant Development at six months of age. VLBW, *Nurse researcher, 45*(5), 291.

Medoff-Cooper, B., & Ray, W. (1995). Neonatal sucking behavior. *Image, 27,* 3, 195.

Meier, P. P. et al. (2000). Nipple shields for preterm infants: Effect on milk transfer and duration of breastfeeding. *Journal of Human Lactation, 16*(2), 106.

Merewood, A., & Philipp, B. (2001). *Breastfeeding: Conditions and diseases, a reference guide.* Amarillo, TX: Pharmasoft Publishing.

Messenger, M. (1982). *The breastfeeding book.* New York: Van Nostrand Reinhold.

Minchin, M. (1985). *Breastfeeding matters.* Sydney, Australia: Alma Publications.

Minchin, M. (1989). Positioning for breastfeeding. *Birth, 16*(2), 67.

Mohrbacher, N., & Stock, J. (1997). *The breastfeeding answer book.* Schaumburg, IL: La Leche League International.

Mulford, C. (1992). The mother-baby assessment (MBA): An "Apgar score" for breastfeeding. *Journal of human lactation, 8:*82.

Neifert, M. (1996). Early assessment of the breastfeeding infant. *Contemporary Pediatrics,* October, 2.

Neifert, M. (1998). *Dr. Mom's guide to breastfeeding.* New York: Penguin Group.

Neifert, M. et al. (1985). Lactation failure due to insufficient glandular development of the breast. *Pediatrics, 76,*823.

Neifert, M. et al. (1995). Nipple confusion: Toward a formal definition. *Journal of pediatrics, 126,* S125.

Niemela, M. et al. (1995). A pacifier increases the risk of recurrent otitis media in children in daycare. *Pediatrics 96*(1), 884.

Nowak, A. J. et al. (1988). Imaging evaluation of the human nipple during breastfeeding. *American journal of diseases of children, 142*(1), 76.

Nowak, A. J . et al. (1994). Imaging evaluation of artificial nipples during bottle feeding. *Archives of pediatrics & adolescent medicine, 148*(1), 40.

Nowak, A. J. et al. (1995). Imaging evaluation of breast-feeding and bottle-feeding systems. *Journal of Pediatrics, 126*(6), S 130.

Nowlis, G., & Kessen, W. (1976). Human newborns differentiate differing concentrations of sucrose and glucose. *Science,* 191(4229): 865.

Nyqvist, K. et al. (1999). The development of preterm infants' breastfeeding behavior. *Early human development, 55,* 247.

Nyqvist, K. (2001). Preterm infants are capable of sucking and milk intake at low postmenstrual age. *The Symposium on breastfeeding research, practice and advocacy,* held in Reykjavik, Iceland on March 20 and 21 by The Healthy Children 2000 Project.

Pascale, J. et al. (1996). Breastfeeding, dehydration and shorter maternity stays. *Neonatal Network, 15*(7), 37.

Pernoll, M. (Ed.). (1991). *Current obstetric & gynecologic diagnosis & treatment.* Englewood Cliffs, NJ: Prentice Hall.

Petok, E. (1995). Breast cancer and breastfeeding: five cases. *Journal of human lactation, 11,* 205.

Post-Birth Partnership of Washington State, A Program of Healthy Mothers, Healthy Babies Coalition of Washington. (1998). *The post-birth partnership: Essential knowledge for post-birth care.* Seattle, WA: Author.

Powers, N. G., & Slusser, W. (1997). Breastfeeding update 2: Clinical lactation management. *Pediatrics in Review, 18*(5), 147.

Prieto, C. R. et al. (1996). Sucking pressure and its relationship to milk transfer during breastfeeding in humans. *Journal of reproduction and fertility, 108,* 69.

Renfrew, M. et al. (2000). *The new bestfeeding: Getting breastfeeding right for you.* Berkley, CA: Celestial Arts.

Righard, L. (1996). Early enhancement of successful breast-feeding. *World Health Forum, 17,* 92.

Righard, L. (1998). Are breastfeeding problems related to incorrect breastfeeding technique and the use of pacifiers and bottles? *Birth, 25*(1), 40.

Righard, L., & Alade, M. (1992). Sucking technique and its effect on success of breastfeeding. *Birth, 19*(4), 185.

Righard, L. et al. (1990). Effect of delivery room routines on success of first breastfeed. *Lancet, 336,* 1105.

Righard, L. et al. (1997). Breastfeeding and the use of pacifiers. *Birth, 24,* 116.

Riordan, J., & Auerbach, K. (1999). *Breastfeeding and human lactation.* (2nd ed.). Boston: Jones and Bartlett.

Riordan, J. et al. (2001). Predicting breastfeeding duration using the LATCH breastfeeding assessment tool. *Journal of human lactation, 17*(1):20.

Riordan, J., & Koehn, M. (1997). Reliability and validity testing of three breastfeeding assessment tools. *Journal of obstetrics, gynecological and neonatal nursing, 26*(2), 181.

Roseman, B. D. (1981). Sunkissed urine. *Pediatrics, 67,* 443 (letter).

Saber, A. et al. (1996). The milk rejection sign: A natural tumor marker. *American surgeon, 62*(12): 998.

Selley, W. G. et al. (1990). Coordination of sucking, swallowing and breathing in the newborn: Its relationship to infant feeding and normal development. *British journal of disorders of communication, 25,* 311.

Sepkoski, A. et al. (1992). The effects of maternal epidural anesthesia on neonatal behavior during the first month. *Developmental medicine and child neurology, 34,*1072.

Shrago, L. (1992). The breastfeeding dyad: Early assessment, documentation, and intervention. *NAACOG clinical issues, 3*(2), 583.

Shrago, L., & Bocar, D. (1990). The infant's contribution to breastfeeding. *Journal of obstetric, gynecologic, and neonatal nursing, 19*(3), 209.

Smith, W. L. et al. (1985). Physiology of suckling in the normal term infant using real-time. *US. Radiology, 156:*379.

Smith, W. L. et al. (1988). Imaging evaluation of the human nipple during breast-feeding. *American journal of diseases of children, 142,* 76.

Springhouse, (1998). *Assessment made incredibly easy!* Springhouse, PA, Author.

Stuart-Macadam, P., & Dettwyler, K. A. (1995). *Breastfeeding: Biocultural perspectives.* New York: Aldine de Gruyter.

Tappero, E., & Honeyfield, M. (Eds.). (1996). *Physical assessment of the newborn: A comprehensive approach to the art of physical examination.* Santa Rosa, CA: NICU Ink, Book Publishers.

Thureen, P. et al. (1999). *Assessment and care of the well newborn.* Philadelphia, PA: W. B. Saunders.

UNICEF. (1999). *Breastfeeding: A foundation for a healthy future.* Geneva, Switzerland: Author.

U.S. Department of Health and Human Services. (1992). *Healthy People 2000 goals for the nation: National health promotion and disease prevention objectives.* Washington, DC: Author.

U.S. Department of Health and Human Services. (2000). *HHS blueprint for action on breastfeeding.* Washington, DC: U.S. Department of Health and Human Services, Office on Women's Health.

VanHeerden, J. A. et al. (1988). Pseudohypherparathyroidism secondary to gigantic mammary hypertrophy. *Archives of surgery, 123,* 80.

Vice, F. L. et al. (1995). Correlation of cervical auscultation with physiological recording during suckle-feeding in newborn infants. *Developmental medicine and child neurology, 37,* 167.

Walker, M. (Ed.). (2002). *Core curriculum for lactation consultant practice.* Sudbury, MA: Jones and Bartlett.

Weber, F. et al. (1986). An ultrasonographic study of the organization of sucking and swallowing by newborn infants. *Developmental medicine and child neurology, 28,* 19.

Wessel, M. (1954). Paroxymal fussing in infancy sometimes called "colic." *Pediatrics, 114,* 421.

Widstrom, A. M., & Thingstrom-Paulsson, J. (1993). The position of the tongue during rooting reflexes elicited in newborn infants before the first suckle. *Acta pediatrica, 82,* 281.

Wiessinger, D. (1998). A breastfeeding teaching tool using a sandwich analogy for latch-on. *Journal of human lactation, 14,* 51.

Wilson, S. L. et al. (1981). Coordination of breathing and swallowing in human infants. *Journal of applied physiology, 50,* 851.

Wilson-Clay, B., & Hoover, K. (1999). *The breastfeeding atlas.* Austin, TX: LactNews Press.

Wolf, L. S., & Glass, R. P. (1992). *Feeding and swallowing disorders in infancy: Assessment and management.* Tuscon, AZ: Therapy Skill Builders.

Wolff, P. H. (1968). The serial organization of sucking in the young infant. *Pediatrics, 42,* 943.

Woolridge, M. W. (1986). The aetiology of sore nipples. *Midwifery, 2,* 172.

World Health Organization. (1990). *The Innocenti declaration.* Geneva, Switzerland: Author.

Ziemer, M. et al. (1990). Methods to prevent and manage nipple pain in breast-feeding women. *Western Journal of nursing research, 12,* 732.

Ziemer, M. et al. (1995). Evaluation of a dressing to reduce nipple pain and improve nipple skin condition in breast-feeding women. *Nurse researcher, 44*(6): 347.

Ziemer, M., & Pigeon, J.(1993). Skin changes and pain in the nipple during the 1st week of lactation. *Journal of obstetric, gynecologic, and neonatal nursing,* May/June, 247.

Zuckerman B. S., & Frank, D. A. (1992). Infancy and toddler years. In M. D. Levine et al. (Eds.), *Developmental and behavioral pediatrics.* Philadelphia, PA: W. B. Saunders.

Videos

Mark-It TV et al. (1996). *Breastfeeding: Coping with the first week*. Bristol, England: Author.

Pakkho, N. (1994). *She needs you*. Gothenburg, Sweden: The Swedish Breastfeeding Institute.

The Royal College of Midwives. (1990). *Helping a mother to breastfeed: No finer investment*. London: Healthcare Productions Ltd.

University of New York, Stony Brook. (1994). *Baby talk*. Farmingdale, NY: Wolf Creek Productions.

Vida Health Communications. (1999). *The clinical management of breastfeeding for health professionals*. Cambridge, MA: Author.

Index

COLOR PLATE 2–1 Breaking the seal prior to removing infant from the breast.

Used with permission. © Healthy Children 2000 Project, Inc.

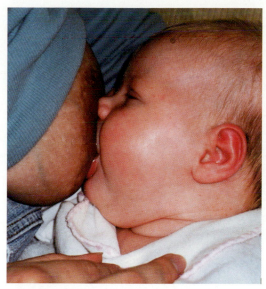

COLOR PLATE 2–2 Bottom lip flanged out and back, upper lip flanged out.

Used with permission. © Healthy Children 2000 Project, Inc.

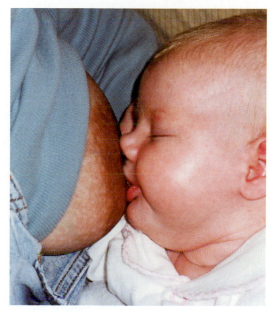

COLOR PLATE 3–1 Narrow gape.

Used with permission. © Healthy Children 2000 Project, Inc.

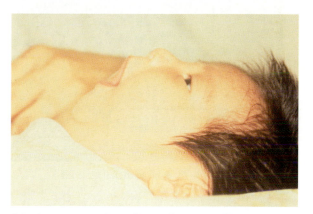

COLOR PLATE 3–2 Infant with very receding chin [mandible].

Used with permission. © Lactation Institute and Chele Marmet

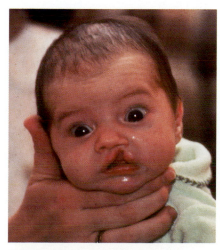

COLOR PLATE 3–3 Infant with unilateral cleft of lip and palate.

Used with permission from Sarah Coulter Danner

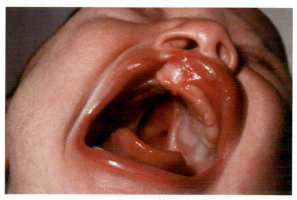

COLOR PLATE 3–4 Interior view—infant with unilateral cleft lip and palate.

Used with permission from Sarah Coulter Danner

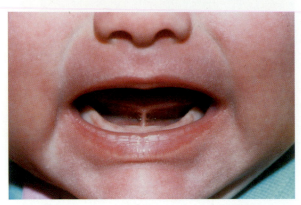

COLOR PLATE 3–5   Infant with tight frenulum.

Used with permission of Kay Hoover, MEd, IBLLC

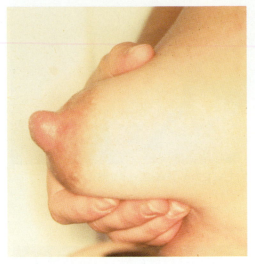

COLOR PLATE 3–6   Angled/beveled nipple, just after breastfeeding.

Used with permission. © Lactation Institute and Chele Marmet

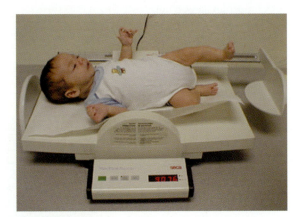

COLOR PLATE 3–7   Precise digital scale for determining breastmilk intake.

Used with permission. © Healthy Children 2000 Project, Inc.

COLOR PLATE 4–1   Infant showing avoidance behavior of finger splaying, arm and leg extension.

Used with permission. © Health Education Associates

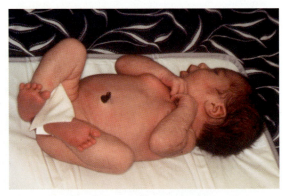

COLOR PLATE 4–2   Newborn: physiologic flexion—13d.

Used with permission. © Lactation Institute and Chele Marmet

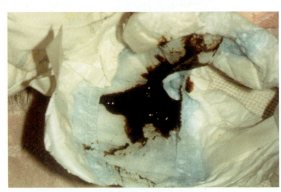

COLOR PLATE 4–3   Meconium in diaper.

Used with permission. © Lactation Institute and Chele Marmet

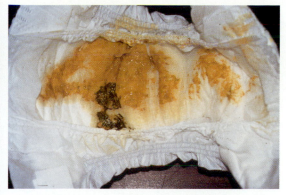

COLOR PLATE 4–4 Transition stool of a 4-day-old, breastfed infant.

Used with permission. © Lactation Institute and Chele Marmet

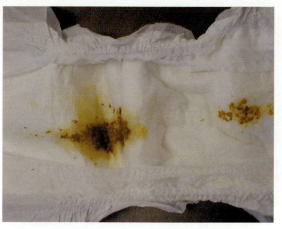

COLOR PLATE 4–5 Normal breastmilk stool.

Used with permission. © Healthy Children 2000 Project, Inc.

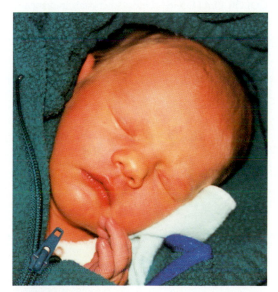

COLOR PLATE 5–1 Jaundiced newborn.

Used with permission. © Healthy Children 2000 Project, Inc.

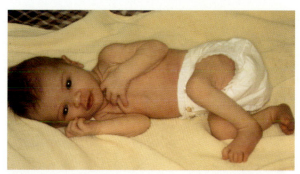

COLOR PLATE 5–2 Poor skin turgor in a 3-week-old.

Used with permission. © Lactation Institute and Chele Marmet

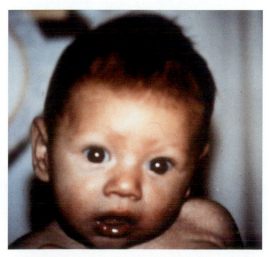

COLOR PLATE 5–3 Cephalohematoma may affect infant's ability to suck correctly.

Used with permission. © Lactation Institute and Chele Marmet

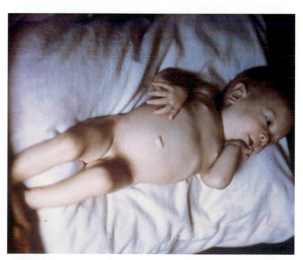

COLOR PLATE 5–4 Hypotonic infant, failure to thrive and feeding problems.

Used with permission. © Lactation Institute and Chele Marmet

COLOR PLATE 5–5   Extreme arching in 2-month-old causing feeding problems and failure to thrive.

Used with permission. © Lactation Institute and Chele Marmet

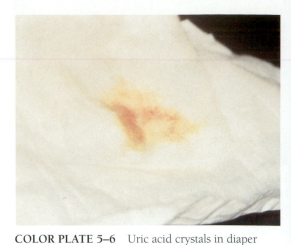

COLOR PLATE 5–6   Uric acid crystals in diaper showing dehydration of infant.

Used with permission. © Lactation Institute and Chele Marmet

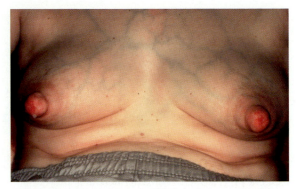

COLOR PLATE 6–1   Veins of breast: lactating mother, 26 weeks postpartum, with prominent veining characteristic of lactation.

Used with permission. ©Lactation Institute and Chele Marmet

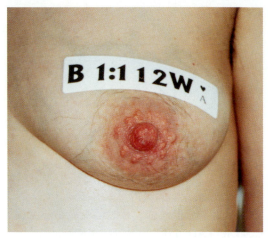

COLOR PLATE 6–2   Prominent Montgomery glands.

Used with permission. ©Healthy Children 2000 Project, Inc.

COLOR PLATE 6–3   From left: colostrum, breast milk, and artificial infant milk (AIM).

Used with permission. ©Lactation Institute and Chele Marmet

COLOR PLATE 6–4   Woman expresses a drop of milk.

Used with permission. © Health Education Associates

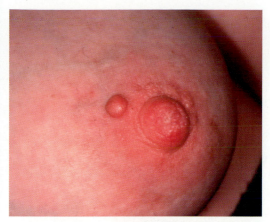

COLOR PLATE 7–1   Super-numerary nipple on left areola.

Used with permission. ©Lactation Institute and Chele Marmet

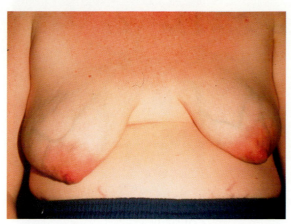

COLOR PLATE 7–2   Insufficient glandular tissue.

Used with permission. ©Lactation Institute and Chele Marmet

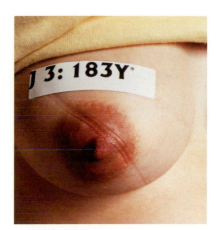

COLOR PLATE 7–3   Indentation mark from a too-tight bra.

Used with permission. ©Healthy Children 2000 Project, Inc.

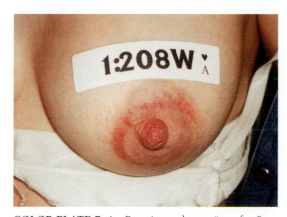

COLOR PLATE 7–4   Reaction to breast "comfort" device.

Used with permission. ©Healthy Children 2000 Project, Inc.

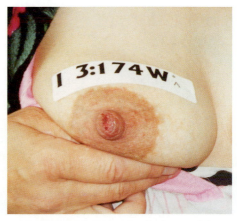

COLOR PLATE 7–5   Nipple damaged from poor latch-on.

Used with permission. ©Healthy Children 2000 Project, Inc.

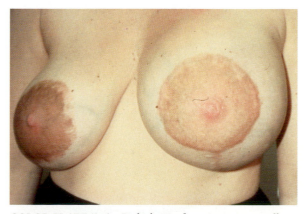

COLOR PLATE 7–6   Right breast functioning normally in spite of implant; left breast painfully enlarged.

Used with permission. ©Lactation Institute and Chele Marmet

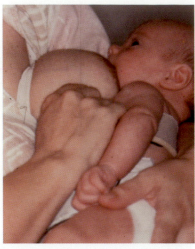

COLOR PLATE 7–7 Very poorly fitting bra is likely to interfere with milk drainage.

Used with permission. ©Lactation Institute and Chele Marmet

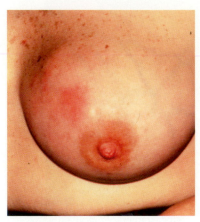

COLOR PLATE 7–8 Abscessed area in left breast.

Used with permission. ©Lactation Institute and Chele Marmet

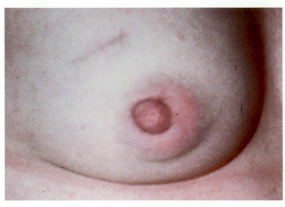

COLOR PLATE 7–9 Nipple off center in mother with breast cancer.

Used with permission. ©Lactation Institute and Chele Marmet

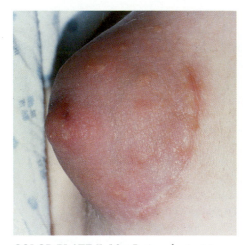

COLOR PLATE 7–10 Periareolar incision.

Used with permission of Kay Hoover, M.Ed., IBCLC

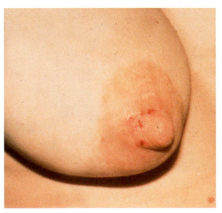

COLOR PLATE 7–11 Herpes on nipple.

Used with permission. ©Lactation Institute and Chele Marmet

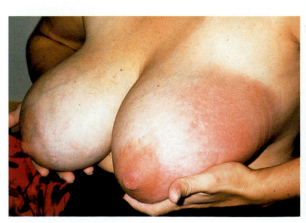

COLOR PLATE 7–12 Unilateral mastitis.

Used with permission. ©UNICEF C-107-39

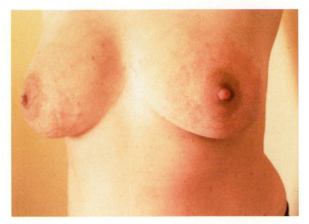

COLOR PLATE 7-13   Contact dermatitis.

Used with permission. ©Lactation Institute and Chele Marmet

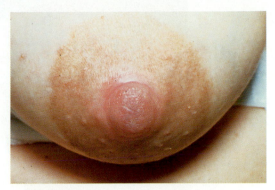

COLOR PLATE 7-14   Pink *candida* sheen and on nipple and areola.

Used with permission. ©UNICEF C-107-33

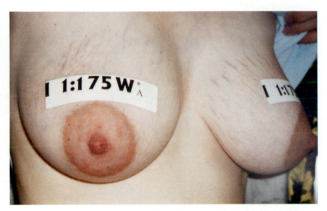

COLOR PLATE 7-15   Stretch marks on the breast.

Used with permission. ©Healthy Children 2000 Project, Inc.

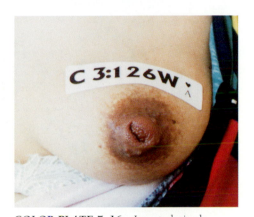

COLOR PLATE 7-16   Inverted nipple before feeding.

Used with permission. ©Healthy Children 2000 Project, Inc.

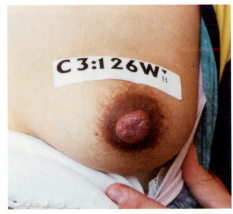

COLOR PLATE 7-17   Inverted nipple after feeding.

Used with permission. ©Healthy Children 2000 Project, Inc.

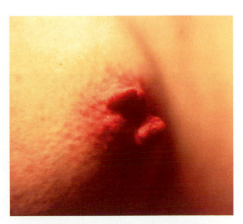

COLOR PLATE 7-18   Raspberry nipple.

Used with permission. ©Lactation Institution and Chele Marmet

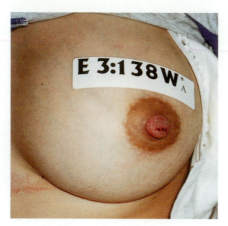

COLOR PLATE 7–19   Cracked nipple from improper positioning.
Used with permission. ©Healthy Children 2000 Project, Inc.

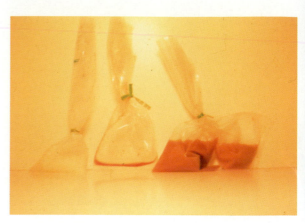

COLOR PLATE 7–20   Rusty pipe milk.
Used with permission. ©Healthy Children 2000 Project, Inc.

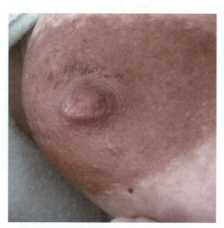

COLOR PLATE 7–21   Nipple with white compression line from small mouth angle.
Used with permission. ©Healthy Children 2000 Project, Inc.

COLOR PLATE 8–1   A selection of breast pumps.
Used with permission. © Healthy Children 2000 Project, Inc.

COLOR PLATE 8–2   A selection of breast/nipple comfort devices.
Used with permission. © Healthy Children 2000 Project, Inc.

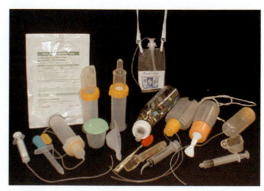

COLOR PLATE 8–3   A selection of infant feeding devices.
Used with permission. © Healthy Children 2000 Project, Inc.